THE MORAL OF THE STORY

Folktales for Character Development

SECOND EDITION

Bobby & Sherry Norfolk

August House Publishers, Inc.
LITTLE ROCK

First edition published 1999 by August House Publishers, Inc.
Second edition published 2006 by August House Publishers, Inc.
P.O. Box 3223, Little Rock, Arkansas 72203
501-372-5450
http://www.augusthouse.com

Interior design and typesetting by Desktop Miracles, Inc.

Printed in the United States of America
10 9 8 7 6 5 4 3 2 1   HC

LIBRARY OF CONGRESS CATALOGING-IN-PUBLICATION DATA

Norfolk, Bobby, 1951–
     The moral of the story: folktales for character development / Bobby & Sherry
Norfolk.—2nd ed.
       p.   cm.
     Includes bibliographical references.
     ISBN-13: 978-0-87483-798-8
     ISBN-10: 0-87483-798-7
     1. Folklore and children.   2. Tales—Study and teaching.   3. Moral development.
4. Personality development.   I. Norfolk, Sherry, 1952–   II. Title.

GR43.C4N67   2006
370.11'4—dc22   2005055566

The paper used in this publication meets the minimum requirements of the American National Standards for Information Sciences—Permanence of Paper for Printed Library Materials, ansi.48–1984.

Foreword

Bobby and Sherry Norfolk take character education, in word and in deed, into a zone of high student engagement and link character education to rigorous academic standards.

Storytelling is a powerful approach, and they not only do it extremely well but teach the rest of us ways to strengthen our capacity to do it. Beyond good advice, the Norfolks "Walk the Talk" and together and separately engage students in meaningful conversations about the right things. They build understanding, skills, and character in ways that are clearly gifted. While most of us can't do it as they do, we are encouraged, more than we are intimidated, to try to do it our own way.

As an end in itself character education is always important. From the earliest times, and seemingly needed more than ever, we need to raise up our children to develop the character traits and habits that will help them to do good, and this book helps us all to be more effective at it.

We also want our children to do well, to be successful in school and in all aspects of their lives. Character education as a means, as a prerequisite to success in different aspects of our lives, is also important. Schools with strong character education initiatives lay the foundation for a quality learning environment, one that encourages students to do well academically.

The current pressure for academic achievement has made it even more necessary to deliberately create a good culture for learning in a school. The historical obligation to help students become good citizens has never been more important.

The practical and idealistic guidance from this book is invaluable in such a climate. It makes clear how to implement fun and interesting ways to develop good character. In addition, Bobby and Sherry tie their methods to solid and well-documented approaches to character education, notably Robert Coles, whom they quote: "Stories from real life as well as stories from the movies, from literature, can stir and provoke the moral imagination. Didactic or theoretical arguments don't work well; narratives, images, observed behavior all do."

Full of great stories, proven methods, engaging activities, and—most importantly of all—full of heart, this work offers just what is needed for our time.

—Dr. Richard Benjamin
Senior Fellow at the RTM Institute for Leadership,
Ethics and Character at Kennesaw State University,
Consultant to The GRAMMY® Foundation / Artful
Learning and Character through Service Learning and
Executive in Residence, Kennesaw State University

Contents

Introduction

"To engage students in the lessons of human character and ethics contained in our history and literature without resorting to empty preaching and crude didacticism is the great skill of teaching."[1]

—KEVIN RYAN

During the 1980s, the moral/ethical issue was at one of its lowest points in America. *Time, Newsweek*, and *U.S. News & World Report* were all asking, "Where have our morals and ethics gone?" This was during the time that Ivan Boesky was indicted, we were experiencing the Iran-Contra hearings, and we were in the midst of the savings and loan rumblings. So Sandy MacDonnell, Chief Executive Officer of McDonnell Douglass Corporation in St. Louis, got together with the CEO of Emerson Electric and CEO of Ralston Purina Company to explore how we could teach moral and ethical lessons without being preachy. The eleven-year-old daughter of the general manager of the local CBS affiliate in St. Louis came up with the answer. She said, "Daddy, we had a storyteller in our school who got everyone excited about reading and learning." They auditioned six storytellers for a pilot television program, and Bobby Norfolk won the audition.

Bobby worked with a puppet named Grouchie Gator, operated by Doug Kincaid. The name of the weekly television show was *Gator Tales*. Every Saturday morning they presented a problem, a problem that Grouchie Gator couldn't solve. The problem was presented not only to the camera but to the seventy-five kids in the studio. When Bobby walked on camera, he listened to an overview of the problem, then he would think of a solution through story. The ratings went sky-high, and *Gator Tales* won three Emmys.

Concurrently, a committee of the Ferguson–Florrisant School District of Missouri was creating a character education curriculum called the Personal Responsibility Education Program (PREP). This committee developed questionnaires that were sent to a pilot group of schools. On Monday morning, teachers distributed the questionnaires to the kids who had watched *Gator Tales* on Saturday. When the results were tabulated in the PREP office, they found out that not only were the kids learning social skills, but their reading skills were increasing as well. At the end of the show, Bobby would send them to the libraries and bookstores to find the books that contained the stories he had told. Many teachers called and told him how the reading levels of their kids had gone up. *Gator Tales* brought storytelling and character education right in your face, right into your home every Saturday morning, against a heavy cartoon lineup.

8

After that, whenever Bobby went to schools to tell stories, he would always explore six character traits, building his stories around self-esteem, responsibility, teamwork and cooperation, respect, honesty, and humanity. Other storytellers were working with PREP as well, and they all learned what storytellers have known for centuries: *storytelling is a powerful tool for educating children about ethics and values.*

PREP continues to successfully teach children in the St. Louis area about those six core values. Meanwhile, school districts all over the country are discovering the need for character education and searching for and developing curriculums to meet those needs. But PREP remains one of the few program to our knowledge that truly recognizes and utilizes the power of story. (Educator Patty Smith, in Midland, Texas, uses twelve core values within their curriculum and sponsors a storytelling festival annually to highlight those values.)

OUR AIMS

This book is for any educator, storyteller, social worker, librarian, scout leader, Sunday school teacher, youth group leader, or parent who is interested in using the art of storytelling to teach moral values and develop good character. While we know that one small book can't provide everything for everybody, our intent is that anyone who picks up this book will find inspiration, motivation, and guidance to meet the needs of the children they serve.

Since tellers work in many styles and formats (just as we do), we have tried to represent each of these styles and formats within the collection of stories we have chosen. We want to show how each of these styles can fit within the context of character education—and to provide choices, rationales, and alternatives. And since most of the storytellers we know who work in educational settings need materials that run the gamut from pre-K through high school, we have provided stories that run that full gamut as well.

The stories published in this book represent only the tiniest tip of the iceberg; they are meant more as examples of what's possible, rather than as a definitive collection. Only you can make the decision about what is appropriate for you and your intended audience, so feel free to tell the stories we share, to explore the bibliography of recommended materials that are listed, and to find your own favorite tales. Then, accept the challenges implicit in Plato's words of wisdom: "But if you ask what is the good of education in general, the answer is easy: that education makes good men, and that good men act nobly."[2]

What is Character Education?

"Moral education of our children is in fact going on all the time, every waking hour of the day and three hundred and sixty-five days a year. Every influence that modifies the disposition and habits, the desires and thoughts of a child is part of the development of his character."[3]

—John Dewey

Moral education is indeed going on all the time. On television, in movies, on the street, children are bombarded with messages: alcohol, cigarettes, and drugs are cool; violence solves problems; the bad guys always win and the good guys are dweebs. Educators see the need to counter these messages with a formal curriculum in public schools, but because the United States is a multiethnic, multiracial nation, many school authorities have despaired of coming up with a shared vision of "the good person" to guide curriculum builders.

The work of C.S. Lewis may provide a multicultural model of a good person. He discovered that certain ideas about how one becomes a good person recur in the writings of the ancient Egyptians, Babylonians, Hebrews, Chinese, Norse, Indians, and Greeks, and in the Anglo-Saxon and American writings as well. Common values included kindness; honesty; loyalty to parents, spouses, and family members; an obligation to help the poor, the sick and the less fortunate; and the right to private property. Lewis called this universal path to becoming a good person "the Tao."[4] Combining the wisdom of many cultures, this Tao could be the multicultural pattern for curriculum developers to follow.

Accordingly, we have searched through many definitions of Character Education, seeking one which most closely matches this Tao. Definitions vary according to the agenda of the person or group writing them, but Thomas Lickona, Director of the Center for the 4th and 5th Rs (Respect and Responsibility) at the State University College at Cortland, New York, says it best for us:

> Character Education is the deliberate effort to develop good character based on core virtues that are good for the individual and good for society. Virtues are objectively human qualities (good for us whether or not we know it); they have a claim on our personal and collective conscience. These virtues include respect, responsibility, trustworthiness, fairness, diligence, perseverance, self-control, caring, and courage. They are affirmed by cultures around the world and transcend religious and cultural differences. They are rooted in our human nature and express our common humanity. Virtues, unlike values, don't change. Justice and

courage, for example, always have been and always will be virtues.

The objective goodness of virtues, and our obligation to uphold them, derive from the fact that they:

- affirm our human dignity
- promote the well-being and happiness of the individual
- serve the common good
- define our rights and obligations
- meet the classical ethical tests of reversibility *(Would you want to be treated this way?)* and universality *(Would you want all persons to act this way in a similar situation?)*

In the absence of virtues, no society can function effectively and no individual can hope to live happily. Not to teach good character based on these core virtues would be a grave moral failure for any society.[5]

The Call for Character Education

There is a broad-based, growing support for values education in American schools. Societal moral breakdown and troubling trends in youth character have made character education one of the fastest growing educational movements in America today. Educators note that it is impossible to teach core curricular content effectively when children are fighting, disrespectful, inattentive, tardy, or absent. In order to learn the curriculum content, children must first be safe to learn.

The support for values education comes from the federal government. In 2003, under the No Child Left Behind Act, the U.S. Department of Education issued contracts to assess the effectiveness of character education programs through "scientifically based research."

Support comes from statehouses, which have passed resolutions calling upon all school districts to teach the values necessary for good citizenship and a law-abiding society. At last count, according to information on the Character Education Partnership website, fourteen states have specifically mandated character education, another fourteen encourage character education through legislation, ten more support character education through State Board of Education resolutions or rule, and nine others have received federal Partnerships in Character Education grants from the USDOE to support initiatives within their states.

Support also comes from local schools, such as Winkelman Elementary School in Chicago, which has for years stressed the values of courtesy and caring through their "Let's be Courteous, Let's be Caring" project.

Support for values education comes from businesses, reform groups, local governments, arts and humanities councils, and, most significantly, from parents. For more than a decade, every Gallup poll that has asked parents whether schools should teach morals has come up with an unequivocal yes.[6]

WHERE DOES STORYTELLING FIT INTO CHARACTER EDUCATION?

TRUTH AND STORY

In the beginning of time, Truth walked naked upon the Earth. His skin was smooth and shining, his body was strong and well-formed, and he walked tall and proud. Everywhere he went, Truth tried to share the great store of knowledge that he possessed.

Each time he entered a village, he would call out, "I am Truth. Come listen and learn from my teachings!"

But no one listened to Truth. Oh, sometimes children came running to sit at his feet and hear him talk, but their parents dragged them away, covering the children's eyes with their hands. Sometimes a young woman was drawn to Truth, looking at him with wonder and listening with awe, but her mother immediately reprimanded her and turned her aside. Young men looked at him with envy and fear and turned quickly away. Old

12

women looked at him with fond, reminiscent smiles, and old men with a look of chagrin.

No one listened.

Truth wandered from village to village, town to town, always with the same reception, and always alone.

One day he came to the house of his sister, Story.

Story lived in a fine and fancy house, surrounded by flowers and ferns, trees and blossoming vines. A wide, shady porch stretched around the house, filled with comfortable rocking chairs, soft cushions and hanging swings. The wide windows were hung with lace curtains and brocade drapes, and stained glass cast rainbows of light across the Oriental carpets.

Story herself sat in a wide wicker chair, dressed in a flowing chiffon gown that shimmered with light and color. Her curling hair tumbled about her shoulders, and was strewn with flowers and ribbons, and her fingers and throat, wrists and ankles were adorned with jewels.

When Story saw her brother approaching, she ran to him in distress.

"Why, Truth, you look awful. So sad and dejected. What's wrong? How can I help you?"

"I don't think anyone can help me, Story. I've gone to every village and town, trying to share my knowledge, and no one will listen. I have such important things to say, Story! But I can't make them listen!"

"You're wrong, my Brother. I can help you—I know just what you need. Come with me."

Story led Truth into her bedroom, where she threw open trunks and hampers and armoires full of clothes, shoes, hats and cloaks.

"Dress yourself, Truth."

Truth was horrified.

"Dress myself in these gaudy things? Oh, Story, I can't! I'd feel so silly!"

But Story insisted, and Truth obeyed. He put on purple trousers made of velvet, a fine linen shirt with billowing sleeves and a quilted vest sewn with glittering jewels. He wrapped a flowing silken scarf around his neck, and hung golden hoops from his ears. He put rings on every finger, a pair of silver shoes on his feet, and on his head he wore a hat with a long curving feather. When he thought he was finished, Story wove ribbons into his hair, poked a flower into his lapel, and hung a satin cloak around his shoulders

At last Story was satisfied.

"Now you are ready," she told him. "Go back to the villages, and see what happens."

Truth felt ridiculous, but he thanked Story and set out once more to enlighten the world.

After one year, he returned to Story's house.

"What happened, Truth?" she asked. "You look much happier than the last time I saw you."

"I really don't understand it, Story, but these silly clothes worked! Everywhere I went, people would gather around and listen eagerly to everything I had to say! It was wonderful, but I'm confused. I still have the same things to say. Why will people listen now to what they rejected before?"

Story smiled.

"Don't you see? No one wants to listen to the naked Truth, but everyone will listen when it's clothed in Story."

—Yiddish Folktale

If we want children to hear and understand and practice the truth about the moral way to behave, then we need to tell stories, not preach truth!

In *The Moral Intelligence of Children*, Robert Coles puts it a different way: "Stories from real life as well as stories from the movies, from literature, can stir and provoke the moral imagination. Didactic or theoretical arguments don't work well; narratives, images, observed behavior all do."[7]

Throughout history, traditional peoples have recognized the role of storytelling in teaching values to children. In the 1930s, anthropologist Morris Opler recorded that among the Apache groups of southern New Mexico, a person who had acted in an inappropriate way would often be chided with the statement, "How could you do that? Didn't you have a grandfather to tell you stories?" Such was the understanding of the power of storytelling in shaping character.[8] The power hasn't diminished in contemporary culture. When our stories show over and over that positive character traits of perseverance, integrity, kindness, ingenuity, and humor are rewarded, we are encouraging children to embrace these qualities. And the power of the story to teach is most fully realized when a tale is told, because the teller reveals in a hundred subtle ways his own approval or disapproval of the actions and events he is narrating. Contemporary children still need stories and a "grandfather" who tells them in order to develop the strong, positive character traits needed for life.

Indeed, many educators today still recognize the power of storytelling in values education. Says Carl Yochum, former coordinator of Ferguson–Florrisant School District of Missouri's Personal Responsibility Education Program (PREP), "Stories often influence the behavioral patterns of young people and hopefully contribute to many long-range, positive character changes in our children."[9] William C. Bennett, author of *The Book of Virtues* and its sequels, says that "stories create moral literacy; they supply examples that tell listeners how to recognize the virtues in the practical world, and they help anchor our children in a world of shared ideas."[10] Kevin Ryan, Director of the Center for the Advancement of Ethics and Character at Boston University, writes that "stories, historical figures, and events are included in the formal [character education] curriculum to illuminate the human condition. From them we can learn how to be a positive force in the lives of others, and we can also see the effects of a poorly lived life."[11]

Thomas Lickona, an international authority on moral development and education, writes that "stories, read or told, have always been among the favorite teaching instruments of the world's great moral educators. Stories teach by attraction rather than compulsion; they invite rather than impose. They capture the imagination and touch the heart. All of us have experienced the power of a good story to stir strong feelings. That's why storytelling is such a natural way to engage and develop the emotional side of a child's character."[12]

EXISTING CHARACTER-EDUCATION CURRICULUMS

All this is preaching to the choir, of course. If you're reading this book, you already know something of the power of story and folktales. But you may need to convince others—school authorities, PTAs, and humanities councils—of the efficacy of storytelling in values education.

Unfortunately, while the educators quoted above believe in storytelling, a review of existing character education curricula indicates that most educators have not as yet made the connection between storytelling, folktales, and character education. We found that many curricula and textbooks espouse the use of children's literature, but only two programs officially include folktales, and only two formally include storytelling. The PREP initiative, mentioned above, recognizes the power of storytelling in its curriculum—and can support its belief in story with statistics that show that some schools' referrals to the principal's office have dropped twenty-four percent and that the number of students who read on or above the national level is rising. The Giraffe Heroes Project, a part of the Giraffe Project, teaches children about the qualities of "heroes" through telling the true stories of people who have "stuck out their necks" to help others. *The Heartwood Ethics Curriculum*[13] utilizes folktales and other literature in teaching good values but does not use storytelling to any real degree.

This lack of insight continues to surprise us. How can educators ignore "the living legacy of a people by which the wisdom of the ages is passed to each new generation"?[14] How can they pass over the old stories which have preserved and passed on cultural values from generation to generation in favor of what Fran Stallings aptly calls "the didactic fluff which is being marketed" today?[15] We think there are a number of reasons. First, educators today are scrambling to be "PC." They are leery of being censored for sharing folktales that present negative stereotypes of minority groups, or too much violence. Of course, you can always assure administrators that among the hundreds of thousands of folktales, there are more than enough acceptable tales from which to choose.

Of course, many folktales do have negative stereotypes and lots of violence. As a storyeducator, you can use these negatives as teaching opportunities, discussing the cultural biases and the historical context of the tale, then relating these to current cultural values. You can also help children develop and evaluate alternative behaviors for the characters in the story. Encourage them to retell sexist stories from a feminine point of view, to provide nonracist depictions of ethnic characters, or to create nonviolent solutions to problems that are solved through force in the story. These activities develop children's problem-solving skills and their ability to imagine results of behaviors.

Second, folktales do not come neatly packaged to teach one specific character trait each. Many lesson plans call for the teacher to explore one trait at a time: Honesty, Responsibility, Respect. These lesson plans require that the materials speak to only that one characteristic—but even the simplest of folktales is more complex than that! We see this as a plus, of course. While you certainly can choose to focus on only one trait, each short tale presents a microcosm that can be explored from several perspectives. A tale as simple as "Bibi and the Singing Drum" (on page 73 in this collection) can be used as a discussion starter on responsibility, sensitivity, empathy, courage, resourcefulness, conscientiousness, forgiveness, trustworthiness, cooperation, and persistence. It provides the opportunity to measure character development in the two older sisters and allows children to compare and contrast characters within a story. And, as mentioned above, it can be used as a springboard for creative problem-solving exercises.

And third, maybe most educators haven't thought of it. In our opinion, the time is right to introduce storytelling and folktales as the primary medium for character education.

Curriculum materials and educational strategies for character education continue to be very much in the developmental and experimental stage. Several institutions, such as the Character Education Partnership, assist educators in developing viable classroom approaches.

Nonetheless, many of the materials in current use repel children with saccharine attitudes and bore them with unrealistic settings, lifeless characters, and unappealing plots, resulting in flavorless pap.

The federal government has awarded multi-million-dollar grants to school systems and RESAs across the country to develop pilot programs in character education. These funds support pilot programs exploring a variety of strategies and resources in an effort to identify those that are most effective.

Character education conferences are offered across the nation on a regular basis: in April 2005 alone, eleven conferences were offered. These conferences explore, expand upon, and assist in the dissemination of new ideas and approaches. Storytelling—an ancient approach whose time has come—should be among the ideas shared!

Our job as storytellers and storyeducators is to demonstrate the effectiveness of storytelling in character education. (To paraphrase a famous line, "Show them, and they will follow.") For example, we are currently privileged to serve on the Advisory Committee and as Arts Partners for Character Through The Arts, a Partnership in Character Education project which the USDOE has praised for its positive impact on participating schools, teachers, and students in Georgia. In these dual capacities, we have been able to demonstrate the power of storytelling in the character education classroom as well as its effectiveness in teaching through the curriculum.

Several years ago, we worked with Dr. Gordon Vessels, one of the leaders in character education in Georgia. As the former Coordinator of the Character Education pilot program in the Atlanta City Schools, he assembled a Character Education Festival of the Arts, featuring storytelling, puppetry, dance, drama, and music. Each school in the program was treated to a day-long festival during which children were exposed to each of these art forms in ways that contributed to character development.

At the conclusion of the week-long festival, Dr. Vessels was completely sold on the power of story. "After this experience," he said, "I believe that storytelling is the primary tool for character education."

Well, we do, too. That's why we've written this book.

I

Getting Ready

Before You Begin

In developing this book, we identified stories that we love to tell and that kids love to listen to, ever mindful of the character traits that a particular story exemplifies. There were literally thousands of tales that would have done just as well, so in the final analysis we simply chose ones which we have used over and over with proven results.

We also have provided ideas and suggestions for extending the storytelling experience into discussions and activities that will help kids "get the message." *By no means do we suggest that you must engage children in these activities* every *time you tell a story.* As Margaret Read MacDonald exhorts, "If you *must* dissect the tale to meet your curriculum's guidelines, please commit this brutality only *after* everyone has had a good time, playing with their birthright—the untrammeled folktale."[1]

We couldn't agree more! Our suggestions are made to help parents, educators, and storytellers identify and explore some of the options available to them for making the content of tales accessible to their listeners. You may want to try some or all or none of the methods, and any of those options is okay. The stories speak for themselves, and they will touch listeners in ways that you cannot know or guess.

If you do choose to try some of the follow-up activities, we recommend that you wait a day or two after you've told the story if possible. For one thing, an immediate discussion may actually lessen the impact of the story, denying listeners the opportunity to process and internalize it "untrammeled" by others' opinions and ideas. For another, you may find that discussions about the story arise naturally, and have a life and direction of their own. These unbidden conversations will be every bit as valuable as the one you had planned—or more so, since they will arise out of questions and concerns that reflect the children's own priorities. Watch and listen for these "teachable moments" when the time is ripe for deeper understanding. Listen carefully and you'll get glimpses into value systems and thought patterns you may not be able to tap into during formal discussion.

When you do engage the students in any of these or other activities designed to capitalize on the power and message of the story, we recommend a Socratic approach to leading the group. In other words, ask "why?"

"Why did you say it's okay for Anansi to steal the beans, Johnny?" probes beyond the easy opinion to the moral issues. Telling Johnny he is wrong will shut him down, and you'll never understand where his opinion is coming from—and maybe, neither will he. Asking him to explain "why" provokes thoughtful discussion, and reveals his moral reasoning. It gets you inside his mind—and once you're in touch with the way he is thinking, you can begin to help him develop his moral reasoning to greater maturity.

That does not mean you don't express what *is* the moral thing to do. As a teacher, storyteller, or parent engaging children in discussions of ethical behavior, you do have the duty to let children know what society agrees upon as "the right thing to do." You must help young people understand that there are certain values—such as honesty, respect, and responsibility—that all of us have legal and moral obligations to honor.

But many problems aren't black-and-white. Children face complex issues, and they have to make decisions about them on their own. A set of dos and don'ts that have no foundation in understanding is not a useful help when those issues arise; the ability to reason and think about moral issues *is*. In order to develop that ability, we must allow children to hear, question, and analyze others' opinions in the safety zone of story. Through that process, they will be empowered to make moral choices independently.

One more caveat: don't expect immediate, concrete results. Storytelling is a powerful tool, but it's not like using a hoe. As Susan

Strauss warns us in *The Passionate Fact*, "When you use a hoe, the result is immediately evident and predictable. A story may take years of stewing in the listener's imagination before the listener says, 'Aha!' and the teller has little control over what message a listener will derive from a story."[2] That's true. We have no way of knowing when—or if—the "aha" will take place, but every once in a while we are privileged to be present when it happens.

Recently, we were teaching a mini-workshop for a fourth-grade class in the Atlanta area when we witnessed an "aha." The students had been told a simple story and led through a visualization exercise to help them "make the story their own." They were then sent off in pairs to retell their "new" story to partners. The classroom teacher and the instructors circulated among the pairs, observing and encouraging participation. When we noticed that the classroom teacher was repeatedly drawn to one particular child, we asked if anything was wrong.

"Oh, no," she whispered, her eyes never leaving that child. "It's just that I've never heard his voice before. He has never spoken in class, not since kindergarten!"

But the boy *was* talking, animatedly and enthusiastically telling a story to his partner. When the class reassembled, we called for a volunteer to tell in front of the entire group, and that child raised his hand first. As he walked to the front of the room, his classmates cheered and his teacher wept a few tears. But he didn't seem to notice. He told his story fluently and composedly, as if this were the most natural thing in the world to him, and then he returned to his seat to thunderous applause.

Now, the teacher told us it was a miracle (so did the principal and several other teachers who had had that child in class). And we later learned that the effect was a lasting one—he continued to talk in class and participate fully from that day on. Well, maybe it wasn't a miracle, but it was certainly an "aha." We don't know *what* clicked for that child that day, but we were privileged to be there when it did.

We tell that story to remind the reader—and ourselves—that "ahas" *do* happen. The plot of the story, or the description of a place, or the sound of a voice, or the tilt of a head may have been the key that unlocked the door for that child. We'll never know exactly what happened, only that it *did*.

For every "aha!" moment that we are privileged to witness, we know that there are hundreds more that we don't get to see: the witnessed moments are only the tip of the iceberg. We may not know when or why or how doors of moral understanding are unlocked for children through our stories—we simply know and believe that they are. And whether or not we are allowed to see the "aha" moments, we "keep on keepin' on."

So . . . share the stories and allow the stories to work their magic. Provide a nonjudgmental space for discussion and exploration, guiding rather than forcing children onto the safe path. Believe that the "ahas" will happen, with or without your knowledge. Then get out of the way, and let the magic begin.

Help! I'm Not a Storyteller!

S ure you are—you don't have to be a polished professional to tell stories!

As we stated in the introduction, this book is not intended for professional storytellers alone. It is for any educator, storyteller, social worker, librarian, or parent interested in using the art of storytelling to teach moral values and develop good character.

We are all storytellers—it's the way that humans communicate, or store and pass on information. Each of us in our own way tells stories every day: about the horrible traffic jam on the way home; about the way the kids acted at the grocery last night; about the great movie we saw over the weekend. It's natural. And we all have the ability to use those same communication skills to tell stories to children. It is not necessary to tell them at the level of a professional (unless you happen to *be* a professional). It is only necessary to communicate.

In *Once Upon a Family,* Jean Grasso Fitzpatrick says it eloquently: "Storytelling that nurtures emotional literacy is best understood as a *communication*, not a performance. The telling of a tale is a ritual moment in the lives of teller and listeners. You meet face to face. You make eye contact . . . together you will make the story your own."[1]

So don't take your storytelling *performance* too seriously. The fact is, many of us have experienced at least one slick professional storyteller who has grown so practiced and mannered in his or her telling that the story itself has become wooden and lifeless.

And don't worry too much about your memory, as in, "I just know I'll forget the whole thing. I have a terrible memory." Storytelling isn't about words. It's about images, and emotions, and sharing those with your listeners. The trick to telling a story isn't knowing every word that

24

is written on the page. The trick is knowing how the characters feel and why they do what they do—then sharing that knowledge and understanding with your listeners.

Here's how to begin. You find a story you like—no, *love*. Once you've found that story you love, you'll find that you are burning to share it with someone—so do it! Read it a few times so that you know what happens first, and next, etc. Then close your eyes, and really visualize those characters—how they look and sound and move. Think about how they feel and react to the events of the story and to each other. Look closely in your mind's eye at the places where the story happens, and take a moment to walk about in those woods or sit in that sunny glade. Then think through the story, reviewing the sequence of events and "telling it" to yourself. Check to see if you've left anything out, then tell it again—out loud this time if possible. Now, go tell someone about your story!

"Telling about" a story is a little different from "telling" a story. It doesn't have the pressure of *performance* behind it: you are simply going to tell someone about the story you have found. If, in the process, you begin to bring the characters to life with voices and gestures, that's a bonus. But at this point, simply allow yourself to vocalize the story to a listener.

After you've "told about" the story, you'll have a good feel for how it works as a told rather than a read story, and you'll want to go back and reread the text to make sure you've remembered the salient points. Then, you're ready to *tell*.

Let the story live as you tell it. Bring your own images and emotions to it. Make a personal connection with the story that will allow your listeners to personally connect as well. Maybe it won't be perfect—you might forget a detail and have to backtrack, or exchange one character's voice for another midstream—but that's okay! It *will* be perfect for you and your listeners.

If you want to learn more about the art of storytelling, there are some wonderful resources that we can recommend. Margaret Read MacDonald's *The Storyteller's Start-Up Book: Finding, Learning,*

Performing and Using Folktales (August House, 1993) is our personal favorite. It gives easy, encouraging instructions that will help you jump right into storytelling and keep afloat. Other good resources include:

Robert Barton, *Tell Me Another: Storytelling and Reading Aloud at Home, at School and in the Community* (Pembroke Publishing, 1986).

Norma J. Livo and Sandra A. Rietz, "Storytelling at Home and School," in *Storytelling: Process and Practice* (Libraries Unlimited, 1986).

And don't forget your local storytelling group. Many communities have storytelling guilds and associations that offer support, guidance, and networking resources. To find out what's available in your area, contact:

National Storytelling Membership Association
116½ West Main Street
Jonesborough, TN 37659
(423)913-8214

http://www.storynet.org

Now, read on, because You Are a Storyteller!

2

The Stories

Vulture Learns the Laws of Nature

Nature's laws are strict, and there is always a penalty for breaking them. In this African-American story, Vulture tries to get around the rules, but he's brought to justice by a wily monkey.

It was summer in the African savanna, and the animals were *hot!* All the animals that could hang out in the muddy river were *plop!* stuck up to their eyeballs in it, snoring in the heat. All the animals that could hang out in trees were up in the high branches and dreaming in the shade of the thick leaves. All the animals that could burrow into the earth were snoozing deep in its darkness.

All the creatures were sleeping except Monkey. He was sitting in some shadowy bushes, watching the sky.

Monkey didn't allow the heat to put him to sleep—he was a simian on a mission. Monkey just sat there looking at the sky, rolling his head back and forth, slowly searching the sky for something.

Finally, he saw it. It was a black dot on the horizon. As the black dot came straight overhead at twelve o'clock, it began to descend. It got lower and lower and lower, and when it was in view . . . it was Vulture.

Vulture had been behaving very strangely for the last few days, and Monkey was curious. He wanted to know what Vulture was up to.

Now, Vulture had a problem. By nature's laws, he was a scavenger, only licensed to eat things that were already dead. Usually, that was okay with him, but not lately. With this heat spell, all the animals were staying in the coolest shelter possible, and nobody was coming out in the open to die. Vulture was just about to starve to death! He was out on a last desperate hunt for carrion, when he saw Rabbit poke his head up out of his hole in the ground.

"*Squawk-squawk-squawk!*" cried Vulture. He landed right in front of Rabbit. "Rabbit! How you doing, Rabbit?"

"Well, I'm hot, of course!" moaned Rabbit. "It's so hot I'm sweatin' all inside my big ol' ears. Whew!"

That gave Vulture an idea. He said, "Rabbit, I'm real sorry you're so hot. Now me, I'm just as cool as can be—as a matter of fact, I just came down here to thaw out. My wingtips and my tailfeathers were getting frostbite up there in the sky. Say, why don't you go up there in the sky and cool off, Rabbit?"

Rabbit answered, "Because I don't have wings, that's why! How can I get way up there?"

"Why, that's easy! Just hop on my back, Rabbit! Come on up in the sky where you can feel the air flow through your hair and the breeze blow cross your knees!" said Vulture.

"For real? Okay!" said Rabbit, and without hesitation, he jumped right on Vulture's back.

Vulture took off. *Swish, swish, swish,* up, up, up he soared. When he got up to about two hundred feet, he leveled off and started riding the currents of air.

"How ya doing back there, Rabbit?" called Vulture.

"Oooh, it's so nice and cool up here! My ears are cooling off. And it's—whoa!—kinda far to the ground, too!"

"All right, Rabbit, hold on. I'm going down for a dive." Then Vulture stopped in mid-air, *screech!* He pointed his beak downward and headed into a dive.

"Yeow! Whooooo Hooooooo!" cried Rabbit.

Vulture went at sixty miles per hour. Suddenly, he banked off to the right. Rabbit lost his grip and fell off.

"Whaaaaaaaa . . . .!"

Splat! Rabbit hit the ground. Road pizza all over the grass. It was not a pretty sight. But Vulture had rabbit stew that night—and Monkey watched.

The next day, Monkey was hiding in the bushes again, looking straight up, searching the sky. Finally, his eyes caught sight of it. It was the black dot on the horizon. The black dot came closer and closer overhead, and when it got to 12 o'clock over Monkey's head, it began to descend. It got lower and lower, and when it was in view . . . it was Vulture.

"Squawk-squawk-squawk!" cried Vulture. This time, he landed right in front of Flying Squirrel, who had just run out onto a branch to take a look at the sky, hoping for clouds.

"Squirrel! Hot day isn't it?"

"Yes, it is," panted Squirrel. "I can't keep my bushy tail cool."

"Well, it's real cool up in the sky. Matter of fact, I just came down here to thaw out a little. Why don't you go up in the sky and cool off?" asked Vulture.

"Now, look, don't start up with me. I might be called Flying Squirrel just 'cause I've got these membranes that let me skim from branch to branch. But I don't have wings. How could I get way up there where it's cool?" Squirrel groaned.

"Why, just hop on my back! Come on up in the sky where you can feel the air flow through your hair and the breeze blow cross your knees!" Vulture suggested.

Squirrel perked up. "Okay!" he cried, and hopped on. Vulture took off, *swish, swish, swish.* Up, up, up he soared. When he got up to about two hundred feet, he leveled off and started riding the currents of air.

"How ya like it back there, Squirrel?" called Vulture.

"I like it a lot! It's nice and cool up here!"

"Well, hold on, Squirrel. I'm going down for the dive." Then Vulture stopped in mid-air, *screech!* He pointed his beak downward and headed into a dive. *Whoooosh!* He flew towards the ground at full speed.

"Yahooooo!" yelled Squirrel.

Suddenly, Vulture banked off to the right and flipped upside down. Squirrel lost his grip and fell off.

"Whaaaaaaaa . . . .!"

Squirrel fell to the ground *Pow!* and hit flatter than a pancake. It was not a pretty sight. Vulture had squirrel soup that night—and Monkey watched.

Third day, same thing: Monkey was hiding in the bushes, looking up at the sky, moving his head from side to side. Then suddenly, he saw it—a black dot on the horizon moving slowly across the sky. It traveled in an arc, and when it got directly overhead at 12 o'clock high, it began to descend. Lower and lower it came. When it got into view, it was Vulture.

Monkey strolled out into the hot sun, looking right pitiful.

"*Squawk, squawk, squawk!*" cackled Vulture. He landed right in front of Monkey.

"Monkey! Hot day, isn't it?"

"Yes, it is," replied Monkey. "I been thinking it must real cool up in the sky, though. Is it cool, Vulture? Is it cool up in the sky?"

"Cool? Why, it's downright *cold*, Monkey. Why don't you go on up there and cool off?"

"Now, Vulture, you see any wings on me? How do you think I can get way up there?" Monkey asked.

"I think you can just hop on my back, Monkey. Come on up in the sky where you can feel the air flow through your hair and the breeze blow cross your knees!" Vulture suggested.

"Would you do that for me? You're on, Brother!" Monkey hopped eagerly onto Vulture's back and Vulture took off, *flap, flap, flap,* into the air, higher and higher until he was up about two hundred feet. He leveled off and started riding the currents of air.

"How ya like it back there, Monkey?"

"I love it, Vulture! It's nice and cool up here," answered Monkey. "And kinda far to the ground, too. Nice view."

"All right, hold on, Monkey. I'm going down for the dive."

All of a sudden, Vulture stopped in mid-air and went into his dive, *whooosh!* Vulture was headed nose first toward the ground at full speed.

"Yahooooo!" yelled Monkey. But before Vulture could bank off to the side, Monkey took his tail and wrapped it around Vulture's neck three times, *thwap, thwap, thwap!* and pulled back hard.

"Vulture, I'm gonna tell you what my mama always told me: you'd better straighten up and fly right!" Monkey hollered.

"Awk!" Vulture gasped as he leveled back off, trying to get air to breathe. Vulture tried to dive again, but Monkey just yanked back harder on his tail and commanded, "Didn't your mama ever teach you about the laws of nature, Vulture? You're supposed to eat *dead* things— and you're not allowed to *make'em dead yourself!* Now, I said you better straighten up and fly right!"

"Awk!" Vulture leveled off again, gasping for air.

Monkey flew Vulture all over the continent of Africa. He looked down on the Serengeti, the Sahara Desert, and beautiful Lake Victoria. He saw the River Nile, the Congo, and the great, grey-green, greasy Limpopo River. He even saw the Pyramids.

Finally, Vulture began to plead, "Monkey, I'm getting real tired. You gotta let me put you down before we fall down outta the sky, Monkey."

"Well, all right, Vulture," Monkey said. "Go down very softly."

Vulture landed very lightly on the ground. "All right, get off!" he croaked.

Monkey unwrapped his tail from Vulture's neck and said, "Thanks for the ride, Mr. Vulture." And he walked away.

From that day on, Vulture abided by the laws of nature. He scavenged for his meals, never again killing, but always waiting for animals to die before he ate them. And he learned another lesson, too: he learned always to straighten up, and fly right!

STORY NOTES

Looking for a discussion starter? Some stories seem to provoke discussion naturally, and this is one of them. As soon as we finished telling the story at a county-run teen emergency shelter, one boy muttered, "Hey, he had to survive, ya know."

There was an immediate chorus of dissent and agreement from the group.

"Hey, he's gotta obey the law!"

"Who cares about the law when you gotta eat? He did what he *had* to do, man."

"No, you can't just go killing and hurting other guys just so *you* can survive. What makes you so important?"

"Law of the jungle, man. Survival of the fittest, ya know?"

There were plenty of other comments, but you get the drift. The group was divided among those who felt strongly that Vulture was in the right, those who felt that he was clearly wrong, and those who sat glancing back and forth, their opinions clearly as undecided as their focus.

Now, this was a group to whom survival was not an obscure concept, but an unfortunate fact of everyday life. Many had survived physical abuse; most had endured emotional abuse. They were kids whose childhood had been robbed from them, and who had often taken care of themselves and younger siblings in situations that would challenge adults.

All of them had seen their parents in trouble with the law; many of them had a record in juvenile court themselves. They were familiar with the courts, and glib in the language of the courtroom. So, we suggested a trial.

Vulture would be the defendant, and we asked the young man whose comment had sparked this debate to play Vulture's role. We appointed a defense team for him, as well as a prosecuting team representing Mother Nature herself. The kids volunteered to play other roles: witnesses to the events, the families of Rabbit and Squirrel, and Monkey (the chief witness). We had a few character witnesses, too, and "expert testimony" concerning evidence found at the scene (bits of. fur and DNA from the feathers). The kids appointed one of their counselors to be the judge, and several were summoned to jury duty.

In the course of the trial, we learned that while Squirrel had gathered and stored nuts to ward off hunger, Vulture had greedily eaten

33

every morsel of every carcass he had found, saving nothing for his family or for emergency situations. We heard testimony from Rabbit's family about how he had conserved energy during the famine, thus reducing hunger as much as possible, while Vulture expended huge amounts of energy and increased his hunger as he flew around looking for food.

We also learned about the hardships Squirrel's and Rabbit's family had endured following their deaths. And we learned about how Vulture's family had had to fend for themselves during the famine, while Vulture ate his ill-gotten gains.

The defense claimed that Vulture could not be held responsible for his actions, since he was clearly deranged by hunger, and they asked for a not guilty verdict based on a temporary insanity plea.

The preparation for the trial and the trial itself went on for several days, but the jury was only out for a few minutes. The jury found Vulture guilty on all counts, and upheld Monkey's sentencing: Vulture and his family would forevermore be held to the laws of nature, and only be allowed to eat roadkill. And Vulture would be obliged to take the little animals for (safe) rides in the sky during the hot season whenever they requested.

Justice is a complex and controversial subject. Approaching it from the fictional perspective of story allowed students to explore from a safe distance, without fear of repercussions or long-term ramifications to any of the parties involved. It helped them look at both sides of the situation in order to determine the just thing to do. By focusing on the underlying nature of the events, these students could appreciate the outcome of the original story—which perhaps made them better able to act justly in their own lives.

SOURCE NOTES

Motifs given are from Margaret Read MacDonald's *The Storyteller's Sourcebook: A Subject, Title, and Motif-Index to Folklore Collections for Children* (Gale, 1982).

This African-American tale is related to Motif K1041.3 *Hare flies on buzzard's back, hits overhead with guitar and holds wings outstretched to glide to earth;* and to Motif A2435.4.5.1 *Carrion as food of vultures.*

A dialect version, as told by John Blackamore, is published by Richard Dorson in *Western Folklore,* v. 14 (California Folklore Society, 1955).

Other variants appear in:

Moritz A. Jagendorf, *King of the Mountain: a Treasury of Latin American Folk Stories* (Vanguard, 1960).

Diane Wolkstein, *Cool Ride in the Sky* (Knopf, 1973).

Anansi and the Pot of Beans

Anansi, the African trickster, always teaches his lessons humorously through negative example. In this story from Ghana, West Africa, Anansi's deceit and greed help us understand the need for honesty and respect.

36

Early one morning when the sun was just awakening, Anansi the Spider awakened also and decided that he wanted to do a favor for Grandma Spider. So he picked up the phone and dialed her number: *ring . . . ring . . . ring . . .* "Hello?"

"Hello, Grandma Spider," said Anansi. "I was just wondering if you had any work for me to do this morning."

"Why sure," said Grandma Spider. "I would like for you to plant some beans in my garden."

"Great, Grandma Spider, I'll be right over!" Anansi hung up the phone and ran to wash himself and comb his long hair before going to Grandma's house. Anansi loved going to Grandma's because she was a great cook, and she always had plenty of food for a growing spider.

When Anansi arrived at his grandma's house, he knocked on the door.

"Well, hello, Grandson," Grandma greeted him with a hug and a pat on the head.

Anansi blushed and answered, "Hello, Grandma."

Grandma Spider and Anansi sat in the living room and chatted for a few minutes before going into the garden. Grandma called that "visiting," and she always wanted Anansi to "visit" with her before he started doing any chores. Soon, though, she took him out to the garden and showed him what she wanted done. Then she went back into the house to fix some lunch for the two of them.

Anansi took the beans and began to drop them into the furrows in the ground he had made, just like Grandma Spider had taught him. The sun grew warm, and then hot, and by noon, Anansi was limp with the heat.

"Whew, it's sure getting hot out here, and I'm getting thirsty." Luckily, Anansi had his hat with him. He took it and pulled the brim down to shield his eyes from the glare of the sun. Then he tucked his beautiful shining long hair under the hat, and continued to work.

Soon, Grandma Spider came out on the back porch with a large pitcher of fresh lemonade and called to him, "Anansi! Here's a cool drink for you, Grandson."

Anansi was grateful for the drink and the chance to rest. "Thank you, thank you, Grandma," he said as he gulped the cold, sweet lemonade.

"Anansi, I've been making your favorite meal," smiled Grandma as she watched him drink. "I soaked some delicious beans last night and put them on to simmer this morning. They'll be ready soon for your lunch, along with some cornbread and yams. You think you'd like some of that, Anansi?"

"Wow, Grandma, I'd love it!" shouted Anansi. He finished his lemonade in one last gulp and went back to his work while Grandma Spider returned to the kitchen.

Back in the kitchen, Grandma Spider searched in the cupboard for her special "bean spices," but found the tins almost empty. She put what little she had into the simmering pot, then called out the window,

"Anansi! I'm low on spices and I have to go to the market down the road to get some more. Will you be okay while I'm gone?"

"Sure, Grandma," he answered. "I'll just be here in the garden."

"Now you stay away from that pot of beans, you hear? The beans are too hot and the pot is too heavy—you understand me, Anansi?"

"Yes, Ma'am, I understand you. I won't go near that pot of beans!"

He kept on planting, passing the window as he worked. The beans simmering in their various seasonings began to give off a most lovely aroma. The scent rose from the pot and drifted across the kitchen, out the window, across the back yard and right into the garden into Anansi's nose.

"Mmmmmmm!" Anansi's nose twitched and his mouth began to water. The scent lured him through the garden, across the back yard, and into the kitchen, where he found himself standing in front of the stove with the pot of beans right under his nose.

"Grandma said not to go near these beans. I'd better get on out of here." He turned and started to return to the garden, but the smell pulled him back.

"Surely it's all right just to SMELL the beans!" he said to himself.

Anansi lifted the lid off the pot of beans and the aromatic steam hit him square in the face.

"Ahhhhhh!" Anansi took a deep breath of the steam. He could almost taste those delicious beans! But almost wasn't good enough. Anansi wanted to taste those beans for real.

"Grandma won't have to know. She'll never miss a few beans."

He found one of Grandma Spider's big spoons and dipped into the pot.

"Ohhhhh!" Anansi blew on the hot beans and carefully tasted them. "AHHHH . . ." He spooned up some more and blew on them . . . sluu-uurp . . . he spooned and blew . . . sluuurp . . . he spooned and blew and slurped up spoonful after spoonful of the beans. "Mmmmmmmmm . . . Ahhhhhhh . . . Ohhhhh . . . uh-oh! Grandma will be coming back soon. I'd better not let her catch me eating out of her pot. How can I take some of these beans back to the garden with me?"

Anansi thought for a moment. "I know! I'll put the beans in my hat and eat out of it, and Grandma won't know! Tee hee," giggled Anansi.

Anansi took off his hat and filled it full of steaming beans . . . Plop! plop! plop! He had just put the lid back on the beans, when suddenly, he heard shouts from the garden.

"Hey, hey! Get out of Grandma Spider's garden!"

Anansi ran to window and saw a flock of birds eating the beans he had just planted, and a group of neighbors chasing them and yelling. The birds flew into the air, veered in a half-circle, and plunged right through the open kitchen window! Anansi ducked and swerved to avoid the birds, and the neighbors came pounding up the back porch to beat on the door.

"Get out of Grandma's kitchen, you nasty birds! Anansi, let us in to help you!"

Anansi was in a panic. He needed help with the birds, but what to do with the beans?

"Anansi, let us in!" The door rattled on its hinges, the neighbors yelled, the birds screeched and flapped, and Anansi looked around frantically. The door rattled again, the neighbors yelled louder, the birds screamed and flopped. Anansi did the only thing he could think to do: he put the hat full of hot beans on his head and opened the door.

In came the neighbors, yelling and screaming and chasing out the flapping birds. When everything was quiet, they turned to see if Anansi was all right.

There stood Anansi with tears streaming down his face.

"Anansi! Did the birds hurt you, Anansi?"

The birds hadn't touched him, but the hot beans had. The hot liquid had seeped through his beautiful hair and onto his scalp. Anansi was sweating and shaking. But he tried to sound cheerful when he said, "Thanks, everybody, thanks! I'm fine. The birds are gone. You can all go home now."

The neighbors looked at Anansi in concern. The tears were still streaming down his face, the sweat was pouring down his brow, and his hands were shaking harder than ever. "Anansi, what's wrong? Why are you sweating? Were you frightened? Were you hurt?"

"No, I, uh . . . I, uh . . . I'm just hot and flustered from dancing. I'm practicing a new routine for a musical, but I have to finish rehearsing now, so you'll have to leave!" The beans were scalding Anansi's head and he couldn't stand still. He danced from side to side and up and down, jiggling the hat on his head.

"Anansi, that's a wonderful dance! Let us watch!"

The beans were blistering Anansi's head. The pot liquor was running down his face. He jiggled and danced until finally he could stand it no more.

"Yooooow!" Anansi shouted as he pulled the hat from his head. Beans went in one direction and pot liquor went in the other. Then everyone stared at Anansi in astonishment—his head was as bald as an egg! The beans had cooked his hair clean off! The neighbors began to laugh, "Tee hee, HA hahahaha!"

"Look at Anansi! He was hiding beans in his hat and he cooked his hair right off his head!"

"HA hahahaha!"

Anansi was so embarrassed that he ran into the garden and hid in the tall grass until it was dark. He stays in the tall grass a lot these days—and he isn't so crazy about beans anymore.

STORY NOTES

This adaptation of Anansi's misadventures is full of action, sound effects, and laughter. It provides an invitation to all tellers to expand their use of body language, gesture, sound effects, and voices in order to bring the story to life, much as the traditional tellers may have done it long ago.

They say that people often have to learn things "the hard way"—and Anansi seems to be a prime example. Perhaps children can benefit from Anansi's mistakes.

Anansi's dishonesty and disrespect for Grandma's instructions leads to a pretty painful lesson for him. How can children relate to Anansi's behavior and to the results?

We usually start our discussion by asking children to review the story, developing a sequential outline on the chalkboard or a flipchart so that everyone has a visual reminder of the events. It might look like this:

1. Anansi wants to do a favor for Grandma.
2. Anansi calls Grandma.
3. Anansi takes shower.
4. Anansi goes to Grandma's.
5. Grandma and Anansi chat.
6. Grandma shows Anansi the work she wants him to do in the garden.
7. Anansi begins to plant beans.
8. Grandma brings Anansi some lemonade.
9. Grandma tells Anansi she's going to the store to get spices and tells him to stay away from the beans.
10. Anansi agrees to stay away.
11. Grandma leaves.
12. Beans begin to smell good.
13. Anansi follows smell.
14. Anansi remembers Grandma's instructions and turns back to garden.
15. Anansi is pulled back by the smell.
16. Anansi takes lid off.

. . . and so on.

(If you have time, it's useful to ask kids to "storyboard" the tale, *drawing* the sequence of events, somewhat like comic strips. This is a good way to help visual learners remember what happens and to provide kinetic learners with stimulus during the telling of the story. It's a great way to get discussion going at home, where the approach being delineated here might be uncomfortably formal.)

Next, we go back through the sequence, asking children to identify the point at which Anansi's behavior changed from respectful and obedient to disrespectful and dishonest.

All children agree that when Anansi actually lifts the lid, he has crossed the line. But they also agree that this is not the real "point of change." There's often a lively debate about whether that comes when he begins to follow the smell (going near the pot, as he was told not to do) or when he allows himself to be pulled back, having reminded himself that he is doing wrong.

The general lines of the debate usually go something like this:

"When he went near the pot, he was disobeying."

"Well, he was, but he didn't do it on purpose. He just kind of "found himself" near the pot of beans. That doesn't count. But when he realized what he was doing and remembered what Grandma had said, then he went back to the pot anyway—*then* he was wrong."

Some children are sticklers for the rules: he went near the beans, consciously or unconsciously, so he was wrong. But most kids will agree that it was the *conscious decision* to disobey that was the turning point.

As we move further into the story, Anansi's behavior becomes more and more dishonest and disrespectful. Having established what the turning point in his behavior is, the discussion turns to a different theme: in each instance, who is Anansi lying to? Who is he showing disrespect for?

It's easy to agree that Anansi is disobeying his Grandma when he goes near the pot and eats the beans. But who else is he disrespecting? When Anansi scoops the beans into his hat, who is he trying to fool (be dishonest with)? When Anansi doesn't help the neighbors chase away the birds, who is he dishonoring? When he tells the neighbors he's practicing a dance, who is he lying to?

As the group identifies the "victims" of Anansi's misbehavior, our task is to help them see that, along with Grandma and the neighbors, there is another victim: Anansi himself. He is not respecting *himself* when he decides to be deceitful and disobedient. He is lying to *himself* when he decides that it's okay to smell the beans, then taste them. He is hurting *himself* when he hides the beans in his hat. And he brings embarrassment and dishonor upon *himself* by all of his behavior.

This is an essential understanding for children to reach: that if you respect yourself, you cannot behave in ways that disrespect others. Conversely, if you behave in ways that disrespect others, you cannot respect yourself.

After we have reached this understanding, we ask the group what ways their peers show disrespect for themselves and others. We get the gamut: cheating on tests, tardiness and absenteeism, lying, stealing, drug abuse, teen pregnancy, dropping out of school, gangs. We ask the kids to tell us how each of these behaviors shows disrespect for self and for others, and help them articulate the fundamental importance of self-respect in determining our conduct.

SOURCE NOTES

Motif A2323.1.1 *Anansi hides beans in hat; dances from heat.*

The stories of Anansi's hat trick appear in several anthologies, and variously explain why spiders hide in the tall grass, why spiders are bald, and why spiders hide in corners. Three of those sources are:

Joyce Cooper Arkhurst, *Adventures of Spider: West African Folk Tales* (Little, Brown, 1964).

Harold Courlander, *The Hat-Shaking Dance and Other Ashanti Tales from Ghana* (Harcourt, Brace, Jovanovich, 1957).

Lila Green, *Folktales and Fairy Tales of Africa* (Silver Burdett, 1967).

Three Billy Goats Gruff Rap

In this hip-hop version of an old Norwegian tale, the three goats teach the troll the importance of generosity and sharing—and the results of being a bully.

This is the tale of some goats and a troll,
And the troll lived under a bridge, ya know.
Well, he guarded that bridge both night and day.
He'd gobble you up if you went that way.
But the grass was greener on the other side,
So the goats decided to give it a try.

The littlest billy goat was the first that day.
His feet went trip trap, trip trap.
"Hey! Who's that trip-trapping over my bridge?"
"Hey, fool, be cool, it's me, you see?"
"I've got a hunch you'll be my lunch!"
"But I'm so small, and you're so tall!
Sit in the shade, you'll be repaid;
There's a bigger billy goat in this parade!"
So the troll let him pass
to eat some grass.

The middle billy goat was the next that day.
His feet went *trip trap, trip trap.*
"Hey! Who's that trip-trapping over my bridge?"
"Hey, fool, be cool, it's me, you see?"
"I've got a hunch you'll be my lunch!"
"But I'm so small, and you're so tall!
Sit in the shade, you'll be repaid;
There's a bigger billy goat in this parade!"

So the troll let him over
to eat some clover.

The biggest billy goat was the last to go.
His feet went **trip trap, trip trap.**
"Yo! Who's that trip-trapping over my bridge?"
"Hey, fool, be cool! I'm big, you dig?"
I've got a hunch you'll be my lunch!"
"I've got two sharp horns to run you through.
I've got four sharp hooves to cut you, too.
So come on up and give it a try.
We'll see which one is gonna get by."

Well, the troll was a fool.
He couldn't be cool.
He tried to fight, but the goat was right.
With his two sharp horns, he ran him through.
With his four sharp hooves, he cut him, too.

Then he went on over to the other side,
Where the grass was greener, and he said with pride,
"That troll was a fool, he couldn't be cool.
He should've learned not to be so greedy.
He should've learned to help the needy."

Then the goats ate grass till they got fat.
Trip trap, trip trap. That's that.

STORY NOTES

Attention please! This story is not just for babies. In the first place, it goes too fast for preschool and primary children to follow, and in the second place, it has messages for the more thoughtful elementary, middle- and high-school crowd. So read on . . .

If you want to get kids' attention, use rap! Not that this is *real* rap, of course, but even those ultra-cool middle-school and high-school kids will sit up and take notice when you tell this fast-paced, rhythmic version of an old nursery tale. The upbeat tempo, the impudent retorts, and the opportunities for posturing and voice play all contribute to a fool-proof three-minute showstopper for any age.

When we tell this story, we always ask the audience to "set the pace" by snapping their fingers in a beat that we demonstrate for them. (This is a participatory action that even high-school kids will join.) Many times, we'll get hip-hop inspired sound effects as well, and that's fine as long as it doesn't overwhelm the words. We've noticed that when this happens, peer pressure usually takes care of it before we have to—the others want to hear the words!

Aside from the obvious discussions that this piece generates on the importance of sharing and the results of being a bully, the story presents an excellent opportunity to talk about *options and problem-solving.* We ask groups to identify the points in the tale when characters have "decision-making opportunities." For instance, did the goats have any option other than crossing the bridge? How else could they have all gotten to the other side? How else could the biggest Gruff have dealt with the troll? What would have happened if they had made different decisions at each of these junctures?

Identifying decision-making opportunities, developing alternatives, and imagining results are vital problem-solving skills. Many kids today don't realize that they have choices: between staying in school and dropping out, between listening to their peers or thinking for themselves, between using drugs or refraining. Teaching them to recognize and examine the choices in stories helps them to recognize and examine choices in their own lives. It helps them to realize that there are always choices—not always easy ones and not always attractive ones, but always choices.

In order to make the right choices, young people must also learn to explore alternatives and outcomes of potential actions. Many kids lack the ability to develop alternative plans (I could drop out of school and get this cool job working at the gas station and pay for my car—or I could stay in school and take a part-time job and save for a car). Nor can they imagine what will happen as the result of their actions (if I drop out of school, I'll probably never get a better job than this gas station for the rest of my life). Since they don't or can't imagine the results, they commit the actions. They watch TV and see violence but don't see the destroyed families, ruined dreams, and hopeless years in prison, so they shoot the gun. They see their peers dying young and don't perceive the chance of reaching old age, so they live their lives as if they are going to die soon. Given the ability to spot options, develop alternative actions, and imagine the results of those actions, they might make different choices.

We also like to explore the value of teamwork and cooperation in this story, especially with grades 3-5. The Biggest Billy Goat Gruff knew that the whole family could only get over the bridge if they worked together, so he came up with a plan. After we talk about this, we often underscore this point by re-telling the story using teamwork and cooperation to make it even more fun. The audience becomes the "Troll Team" and rehearses the troll's two lines: "Who's that trip-trapping over my bridge?" and "I have a hunch you'll be my lunch." We signal the first line with one upheld finger, the other line with two upheld fingers. The teller becomes the "Goat Team," and we tell the story again, signaling the "Troll Team" for their part. The story is even better with more than a hundred troll voices booming out the lines!

SOURCE NOTES

Motif K553.2 *Three Billy Goats Gruff.*

"The Three Billy Goats Gruff" is an old Norwegian folktale that has been retold for hundreds of years. This hip-hop version is by Sherry Norfolk. About six years ago, she woke up one morning with the words to this rap version streaming through her mind—and got up and wrote them down as soon as possible so as not to forget. The words haven't changed in the intervening years, but the telling has evolved into a tandem telling with Bobby, and the story has become a favorite with audiences from Alaska to Northern Ireland.

The Tailor

WITH THANKS TO MOLLY KINNEY AND KAREN SELINGER

---

*Based on an old Yiddish song, this participatory tale high-
lights the persistence of a talented tailor and shows that
those who never give up can make something valuable out
of almost anything.*

Once upon a time there was a man named Tesoro who was the
very best tailor in the whole world. He made clothes for kings
and queens, for movie stars and rock stars—even for super heroes! His
stitches were so tiny that they were almost invisible; his patterns fit as
closely as second skin; his fabrics were the finest, the softest, and the
most durable to be found.

But he himself wore rags. His shirts had holes in the cuffs, his jack-
ets had holes in the elbows, and his pants had holes in the seat. He was
a very bad advertisement for his wares.

His wife begged, "Please, Tesoro, make yourself a suit of clothes that
will show people how finely you sew!" His children pleaded, "Daddy,
don't embarrass us so!" But it was no use.

"I will make myself new clothes only when I find fabric that suits
me," Tesoro would answer. And then he would describe that fabric: "It
will be dark as night but all the colors of the rainbow; strong as iron
but light as a feather; warm as wool but cool as cotton."

"Then you will be naked before you make yourself new clothes!" his
family wailed. But it was no use. Tesoro waited for the perfect fabric to
arrive.

And one day, a bolt of fabric was delivered to Tesoro's shop that was dark as night but all the colors of the rainbow; strong as iron but light as a feather; warm as wool but cool as cotton.

"This is it!" cried Tesoro. "Now, I will make myself a coat that goes from the tip of my chin to the tips of my toes."

And he got out his scissors	*Make scissors motion with your fingers. Wait for children to join you before you continue.*
and he cut: Shhh, shhh, shhh.	*"Snip" in rhythm with the sounds.*
Then he got out his sewing machine	*Hold fingers of each hand held flat and parallel to floor.*
and he sewed: Ch-ch-ch, ch-ch-ch, ch-ch-ch	*"Push" your hands gently forward in rhythm with the sound.*
And he finished it off with a needle and thread: Pssst, T! Pssst, T! Pssst, T! T!	*With thumb and forefinger together, other three fingers held aloft, dip your thumb and forefinger in a sewing motion in rhythm with the sounds.*
Tesoro had made a beautiful coat! It went from the tip of his chin to the tips of his toes. He put it on immediately, and he liked it so much that he wore it here,	*Make large arcing gesture with left hand.*
he wore it there,	*Make large arcing gesture with right hand.*
he wore it *everywhere*,	*Make large arcing gesture with both hands.*
until it was all worn out.	*Brush hands down length of body rhythmically with the words.*

At least, he thought it was all worn out, until he took it off and looked at it, realllly looked at it, and found there was enough good fabric left to make a jacket.	*Pretend to hold garment in front of you and inspect it closely.*
So he got out his scissors	*Make scissors motion with your fingers. Wait for children to join you before you continue.*
and he cut: Shhh, shhh, shhh.	*"Snip" in rhythm with the sounds.*
Then he got out his sewing machine and he sewed:	*Hold fingers of each hand held flat and parallel to floor.*
Ch-ch-ch, ch-ch-ch, ch-ch-ch	*"Push" your hands gently forward in rhythm with the sound.*
And he finished it off with a needle and thread: Pssst, T! Pssst, T! Pssst, T! T!	*With thumb and forefinger together, and other three fingers held aloft, dip your thumb and forefinger in a sewing motion in rhythm with the sounds.*
Tesoro had made a beautiful jacket! He wore it here,	*Make large arcing gesture with left hand.*
he wore it there,	*Make large arcing gesture with right hand.*
he wore it *everywhere*,	*Make large arcing gesture with both hands.*
until it was all worn out.	*Brush hands down length of body rhythmically with the words.*

At least, he thought it was all worn out, until he took it off and looked at it, realllly looked at it, and found there was enough good fabric left to make a vest.	*Pretend to hold garment in front of you and inspect it closely.*
So he got out his scissors	*Make scissors motion with your fingers. Wait for children to join you before you continue.*
and he cut: Shhh, shhh, shhh.	*"Snip" in rhythm with the sounds.*
Then he got out his sewing machine and he sewed:	*Hold fingers of each hand flat and parallel to floor.*
Ch-ch-ch, ch-ch-ch, ch-ch-ch	*"Push" your hands gently forward in rhythm with the sound.*
And he finished it off with a needle and thread: Pssst, T! Pssst, T! Pssst, T! T!	*With thumb and forefinger together, and other three fingers held aloft, dip your thumb and forefinger in a sewing motion in rhythm with the sounds.*
Tesoro had made a beautiful vest! It went from the tip of his chin to the tips of his toes. He put it on immediately, and he liked it so much that he wore it here,	*Make large arcing gesture with left hand.*
he wore it there,	*Make large arcing gesture with right hand.*
he wore it *everywhere,*	*Make large arcing gesture with both hands.*
until it was all worn out.	*Brush hands down length of body rhythmically with the words.*

52

At least, he thought it was all worn out, until he took it off and looked at it, realllly looked at it, and found there was just enough good fabric left to make a cap.

Pretend to hold garment in front of you and inspect it closely.

So he got out his scissors

Make scissors motion with your fingers. Wait for children to join you before you continue.

and he cut: Shhh, shhh, shhh.

"Snip" in rhythm with the sounds.

Then he got out his sewing machine and he sewed:

Hold fingers of each hand held flat and parallel to floor.

Ch-ch-ch, ch-ch-ch, ch-ch-ch

"Push" your hands gently forward in rhythm with the sound.

And he finished it off with a needle and thread: Pssst, T! Pssst, T! Pssst, T! T!

With thumb and forefinger together, and other three fingers held aloft, dip your thumb and forefinger in a sewing motion in rhythm with the sounds.

Tesoro had made a beautiful cap! It was a (insert name of local baseball team) cap! He put it on immediately, and he liked it so much that he wore it here,

Make large arcing gesture with left hand.

he wore it there,

Make large arcing gesture with right hand.

he wore it *everywhere,*

Make large arcing gesture with both hands.

until it was all worn out.

Brush hands down length of body rhythmically with the words.

At least, he thought it was all worn out, until he took it off and looked at it, realllly looked at it, and found there was just enough good fabric left to make a button.

Pretend to hold garment in front of you and inspect it closely.

So he got out his scissors

Make scissors motion with your fingers. Wait for children to join you before you continue.

and he cut: Shhh, shhh, shhh.

"Snip" in rhythm with the sounds.

Then he got out his sewing machine and he sewed:

Hold fingers of each hand flat and parallel to floor.

Ch-ch-ch, ch-ch-ch, ch-ch-ch

"Push" your hands gently forward in rhythm with the sound.

And he finished it off with a needle and thread: Pssst, T! Pssst, T! Pssst, T! T!

With thumb and forefinger together, and other three fingers held aloft, dip your thumb and forefinger in a sewing motion in rhythm with the sounds.

Tesoro had made a beautiful button! He put it on immediately, and he liked it so much that he wore it here,

Make large arcing gesture with left hand.

he wore it there,

Make large arcing gesture with right hand.

he wore it *everywhere,*

Make large arcing gesture with both hands.

until it was all worn out.

Brush hands down length of body rhythmically with the words.

54

At least, he thought it was all worn out, until he took it off and looked at it, realllly looked at it, and found there was enough good fabric left to make a story:

Pretend to hold garment in front of you and inspect it closely.

So he got out his scissors

Make scissors motion with your fingers. Wait for children to join you before you continue.

and he cut: Shhh, shhh, shhh.

"Snip" in rhythm with the sounds.

Then he got out his sewing machine and he sewed:

Hold fingers of each hand held flat and parallel to floor.

55

Ch-ch-ch, ch-ch-ch, ch-ch-ch

"Push" your hands gently forward in rhythm with the sound.

And he finished it off with a needle and thread: Pssst, T! Pssst, T! Pssst, T! T!

With thumb and forefinger together, and other three fingers held aloft, dip your thumb and forefinger in a sewing motion in rhythm with the sounds.

Tesoro had made a beautiful story! he told it here,

Make large arcing gesture with left hand.

he told it there,

Make large arcing gesture with right hand.

he told it *everywhere,*

Make large arcing gesture with both hands.

And because it was a story, it will never be All Worn Out.

Story Notes

The story of the resourceful tailor has been retold many times, but our favorite versions always take advantage of the repetitiveness and predictability of the plot to involve the children physically, mentally, vocally, and emotionally in the story. The participatory sequence in this version, developed by children's librarians in Ft. Lauderdale, Florida, accomplishes these goals with humor and style!

Not completely sold on the virtues of participatory telling? Let us digress for a moment to discuss the advantages. You see, educational psychologists tell us that children learn in different ways. Some are *auditory learners* who learn best from hearing and repeating information. Others are *visual learners* who learn best from seeing it—either in print or in pictures or acted out. And still others are *kinetic or haptic learners* who learn best when moving and doing. Most of us learn best with a combination of these behaviors, but each of us has a dominant learning style. Participatory telling can help you, the storyteller, meet the learning needs and provide successful experiences for each child.

In this story, for example, the auditory learners hear and repeat the words and sound effects, while the visual learners see the gestures and facial expressions, and the kinetic learners act out the story. All children are participating at a mental level, creating images and experiencing the emotions that the story evokes. All can choose participatory options that are comfortable and appropriate for them, and can therefore have successful and meaningful story experiences.

The word "options" is important, because your listeners should be *encouraged* to participate, not *forced;* nor should they be made to feel uncomfortable about their choices. The comfort zone can be further extended by allowing children to pick up the participatory parts naturally, within the story, rather than trying to teach the sequences before you begin, which can be overwhelming for many kids. When you reach the part of the story when the tailor picks up the scissors for the first time, make them with your hand as you say the words "so he got

56

out his scissors," then pause and ask, "will you get your scissors out, please?" then wait expectantly until most scissors have appeared before you continue, "and he cut, sh, sh, sh. Then he got out his sewing machine (pause as you make the motion until everyone follows suit) and he sewed. Ch-ch-ch, ch-ch-ch, ch-ch-ch." You'll find that these are all the "instructions" you'll need—simply a clear invitation to join in.

As children chant and gesture along with the storyteller, they also are *learning* the story. Most kids are "telling" the entire story along with the teller by the third or fourth sequence—even if they always seem surprised by the ending.

This ability to learn the story helps children to internalize the meaning. The very repetitiveness of the tale emphasizes the patience and persistence of the tailor, and also underscores the lesson of recycling.

We usually introduce this story very briefly by saying that it is about a tailor who was very persistent. (Persistence is one of the "personal virtues" taught in the Atlanta schools, and even first graders know what it means.) Afterwards, teachers or storytellers can lead a discussion about the ways in which Tesoro exhibited persistence.

In discussion, children are quick to point out that the tailor didn't give up—he patiently waited for just the right fabric, then persisted in finding ways to recycle the fabric as long as possible. Children often insist that the tailor was stubborn, too, providing a good chance to discuss the relationship between stubbornness and persistence and between stubbornness and idealism.

The tailor exhibits other qualities as well: he is hard-working, creative, skillful, flexible, resourceful, and determined. What would have happened if Tesoro lacked any one of the these qualities? Would the story have been the same? Would the story have happened at all? For instance, if he had not been resourceful, he probably wouldn't have seen the possibilities for continued use of the fabric: "He would've just thrown the whole thing away and gone around in tatters again!" one second grader said in disgust. But another countered, "No, he would've just kept wearing it while he waited for another bolt of fabric just like it to arrive; then he would've started all over again." "Wow, what a waste!" Some children decided that his *wife* would have thought of cutting the coat down and making a jacket. That way, the sequence could be left intact.

This tale can be an excellent jumping-off place for a unit on recycling and respect for our environment. Encourage the class to rewrite the story using other materials that can be recycled, such as wood or glass. Working in small groups to accomplish this produces the best results, and requires that the children be like Tesoro: creative, resourceful, persistent, patient, and determined, in order to create a logical story. They also have to be cooperative, respectful of each others' ideas, and willing and able to compromise. This cooperative learning provides an "experiential" approach to character education, teaching children that they can accomplish more together than they can do alone. That is a vital part of moral education.

SOURCE NOTES

Motif Z49.24.1 *Tailor makes increasingly small items from piece of cloth.*

We first came across "The Tailor" as the title story of *Just Enough to Make a Story: a Sourcebook for Storytelling*, by Nancy Schimmel (Sisters' Choice Press, 1978). Basing his work on a Yiddish folksong called "I Had a Little Coat," Steve Sanfield has published a picturebook version called *Bit by Bit* (Philomel Books, 1995). We recently heard it told in Derry, North Ireland, by British storyteller Marion Oughton, who set it in modern-day Derry and involved the audience in "sewing" the various items along with her.

The Dancing Hyena

The opposite of fear isn't fearlessness—it's courage. This West African story demonstrates not fearlessness but courage in the face of danger. It also shows how persistence, responsibility, and ingenuity help solve even very dangerous problems.

After Rooster and Hen were married, they went to live and work on an isolated farm, far away from the nearest village. At first Hen was happy, because she loved her husband and enjoyed making a home for him and sharing the events of the day with him. Every evening, when Rooster came in from the fields, they would eat a big meal; then Rooster would sing and play his mbira for her as she cleaned up the hut and prepared for bed.

But after awhile, Hen missed her family.

You see, she came from a *big* family! She had a mother and father, of course, and she had fourteen brothers and twelve sisters. She had twenty-seven aunts and thirty-two uncles, and seventy-eight cousins and one hundred and twenty-four nephews, and ninety-nine nieces. And four grandparents and eight great-grandparents. She missed them all.

One morning, Hen was so unhappy that she couldn't get out of bed. She lay with her eyes closed, tears streaming down her face.

"What's wrong, Hen?" her husband exclaimed. "Why are you crying? Are you sick? Can I help you?"

"No, my dear husband, I'm not sick," she replied. "I'm lonesome! *I miss my mama!*" And she cried aloud until poor Rooster thought her heart would break.

"No, no, there's no need to cry! You don't have to be lonely. You can go and visit your family anytime you wish!" he told her.

"I can?" she asked tearfully, sitting up in bed and wiping her eyes.

"Of course you can. You can go today, if you wish."

"I *can*?"

"You *can*. Go now, and give my regards to your family."

Hen jumped out of bed and got dressed as quickly as she could.

"Oh, I can't wait. I'm going to see my mama and my daddy and my sisters and my brothers and my cousins and my nieces and my nephews and . . . "

"Yes, yes, you'll get to see your family. Stay as long as you need to, my dear. I'll be all right for a little while without you, although you know that I will miss you all the time you are gone."

"I'll miss you, too! But I'm so excited! I'm going to see my mama and my daddy and my sisters and my brothers and my cousins and my nieces and my nephews and . . . "

"Right. Now get started, while the sun is still cool and the day is long."

The two walked outside together, and to the beginning of the path that led away from the farm.

"Now remember one thing, my dear," cautioned Rooster. "You will soon come to a fork in the path. One way goes straight through flat-lands and meadows. That is the shortest, easiest way. The other goes through dark forests and crosses a swamp. That way is much harder. But you must promise me that you will take the path through the for-est, for that is the *safest* way. I have heard that a hyena waits on the other path, and he will surely eat you up! You must take the path through the forest, do you understand?"

"Yes, yes, of course I understand. Take the path through the forest. I will, I will, oh, I'm going to see my mama, I'm going to see my mama!" and Hen ran off singing and waving until she was out of sight. "I'm going to see my mama, I'm going to see my mama!"

Rooster watched her go, and as he watched, he reached into his big pocket and pulled out his mbira, which he always kept at his

60

side. He thumbed the mbira, playing soft music as his wife danced and sang down the road. When she was out of sight, he turned and went into the fields to work. He smiled as he thought of Hen's happiness in seeing her family, and was glad that he could give her that happiness.

But soon, Rooster began to get a funny feeling, right down in the pit of his stomach.

"Something isn't right," he thought. "Something dreadful is going to happen; I can feel it right here in the pit of my stomach. You know, Hen was so excited about going to see her family, I don't think she heard a word I said. I bet she will take the easy, short path through the flatlands and the meadows. I have to go find out!"

He threw down his hoe and ran down the path to the fork in the road. In the dust, he could see Hen's footprints. Sure enough, they turned down the path towards the flatlands.

"Oh, no! I *knew* she was too excited to listen to me. I have to go help her!"

Rooster ran as fast as he could until he came to a bend in the path. There was a large boulder at the bend, and he stepped behind it, peering out and around to see what lay before him.

And sure enough, there was his wife. And on the other side of his wife was a mean-looking, nasty-looking, *hungry*-looking hyena!

Hyena was moving step by step closer to Hen. And Hen was moving step by step away from Hyena.

"HEEEEEAAAAAHHHWWWLLLLLL!" Hyena screeched. Hen jumped and Rooster drew back behind his rock to think.

"What can I do? I don't have any weapons!" He looked around for a big rock to throw, but the ground was bare. "All I have is my mbira! I guess I could *throw* the mbira, but it wouldn't be enough to stop a hungry hyena!"

Rooster took the mbira out of his pocket and stared at it.

"Perhaps it *will* be enough to stop a hungry hyena," he said thoughtfully. Then he begun to strum softly on the metal keys of the instrument as he moved slowly out into the path.

As he played, the hyena stopped moving forward. He cocked his head from side to side to listen, then he began to sway gently back and forth in time to the music. Hen stayed frozen in place, not moving an inch, as Rooster continued to play and the hyena continued to sway.

Then, Hyena began to dance, lifting his ugly paws and swinging his tailend; turning in circles and leaping into the air.

When Rooster saw that Hyena was totally entranced by the music, he called softly to his wife, "Run, my dear! Run as fast as you can for home!"

And Hen turned and ran as fast as she could for the safety of the farm.

Now Rooster was alone with the dancing hyena.

He kept playing the mbira, and the Hyena kept dancing. But his pinfeathers were getting sore and tired . . . sore and tired . . . sore and tired. The music got slower . . . and slower . . . and slower . . . and stopped.

"HEEEEAAAAHHHWWWWLLLL!" Hyena stopped dancing and lunged towards Rooster.

Rooster began to play again, faster and livelier than ever before. Hyena danced again, spinning and jumping to the rhythm and melody.

But Rooster's pinfeathers got sorer and tireder . . . sorer and tireder . . . sorer and tireder. The music got slower . . . and slower . . . and slower . . . and stopped.

"HEEEEAAAAWWWWWLLLL!" Hyena leaped towards Rooster. Rooster played frantically, ignoring the pain. But soon the music got slower . . . and slower . . . and slower . . .

"I have to think of some way to get away from this hyena," thought Rooster. "My pinfeathers hurt so much that soon I won't be able to play at all. Then the hyena will surely eat me. What on earth can I do?"

He looked around and saw the boulder he had hidden behind earlier. "Maybe I can leap behind the boulder and get away before the hyena figures out what I'm doing," he thought.

So he took a step back towards the boulder. Hyena danced a step closer to him.

He took another step back towards the boulder. Hyena danced another step closer to him.

The Rooster moved back, and the hyena moved closer, until Rooster was right up against the boulder—and the hyena was right up against *him.*

"Well, *this* isn't going to work," he thought. He stood there between the boulder and the hyena, playing the mbira as best he could while the hyena swayed and swung.

Just then, a small rabbit peaked out of a hole at the base of the boulder.

"Looks like you've got a problem," whispered the rabbit.

"I do!" Rooster whispered back. "I do! If I stop playing this mbira, Hyena will eat me up. But my pinfeathers are so sore and tired that I can't play much longer."

"I think I can help you, if you will give me your mbira."

"Anything!" and Rooster slowly placed the mbira in the rabbit's hands, playing all the while. The rabbit took the mbira, continuing the music without missing a beat, and the hyena continued to dance.

"Now run!" Rabbit said. "Run as fast as you can for home!"

And Rooster ran as fast as he could for the safety of the farm.

Now Rabbit was alone with the dancing Hyena.

He played waltzes and jigs. He played rock 'n' roll and he played the blues. And Hyena danced and danced and danced. But finally, the rabbit grew tired of the music and the dancing. He kept playing, but he inched closer to his hole at the base of the boulder. Hyena danced closer . . . the rabbit inched closer . . . Hyena danced closer . . . the rabbit disappeared down the hole!

Hyena stopped dancing. He rubbed his eyes. He turned all the way around, looking confusedly in all directions.

"What's going on here? First, there was a hen there, and I was gonna eat her up!" He smacked his lips, and looked around again.

"Then, there was a rooster there, playing the mbira. And I was gonna eat *him* up!" He licked his lips, looking from side to side.

"Then, there was a rabbit there playing the mbira, and I was gonna eat *him* up." Hyena walked in a circle, searching for the rabbit.

"And now, there's just the mbira." He picked up the mbira and sniffed it, then licked it. "*Blah*! I can't eat the mbira!" He struck it with his paw. "And I can't *play* the mbira . . . so I guess that . . . is the end . . . of that."

And it was.

STORY NOTES

We rarely have to face hungry hyenas, but other kinds of predators, problems, and challenges await us in everyday life. How can the story of the rooster and the hyena help us learn to deal with those dangers courageously and wisely?

Courage can be a difficult concept to talk about: it is a personal thing, embarrassing to lack, sometimes hard to recognize in oneself. But kids are often more willing to speak openly about characters they meet in a story than they are to talk about themselves.

We like to start the discussion by asking students to talk about Rooster. Was he courageous, or just stupid, to go to his wife's rescue without a weapon? What about the rabbit? Was *he* courageous or did the fact that he knew he could escape from danger keep him from being defined as courageous? What *is* courage anyway?

To answer that, we ask students to name someone with courage. Their first answers often reflect our TV and movie culture: they cite "heroes" who are not afraid of anything, like the protagonist in *Die Hard*, or who kill every living thing in sight with arsenals of weapons. But after the first barrage, someone usually points out that those characters aren't being courageous, just macho and stupid.

True courage, students often suggest, is shown when people know and fear the danger, yet don't run from it, ignore it, or allow the fear to paralyze them. We discuss war heroes and firemen and policemen who live with, but are not overwhelmed by, constant fear.

Then, the discussion turns to courage in everyday life.

We ask the students to name someone they *know* who is courageous—not actors playing a part on the screen, or characters in a book, or even people in history, but people they actually know. Turning the spotlight on those in their own lives is awkward and difficult for young people—they will joke around and name themselves and each other with heavy sarcasm.

But that spasm will pass. With a little guidance, students will begin to name people who face serious illnesses like AIDS or cancer, or others who live in gang-infested areas or homeless shelters. They may name parents who are starting new careers or going back to school, brothers or sisters who are disabled, grandparents who are dying. With a little encouragement, almost everyone can name a person in his or her life who faces adversity with courage and dignity.

Now the questioning turns inward: has there been a time in the young people's own lives when they themselves were courageous? (We don't call on anyone or force anyone to answer. This question is posed to give people the chance to examine and evaluate how they have dealt with adversity. A few kids might share a story about themselves, or even tell one about a classmate who was courageous, but that's a bonus. We do recommend that you encourage students to write about their own courageous moments or those of an acquaintance as part of a journaling exercise. The act of writing these thoughts down helps to give them weight and reality for the young people.)

Whenever possible, we recommend that this discussion be followed by some real-life encounters with courage. For example, if there is a disabled person willing to discuss his or her life with the class, or a homeless mother who can describe what her family faces, such people can deepen the class's understanding of what real courage is.

Even better, design a long-term class project, adopting a children's shelter or a senior center. Visiting with the residents, observing their challenges and how they face them, is inspiring. As children begin to recognize the courage with which ordinary people confront their problems, they learn to respect, admire, and value those people. By creating opportunities for youngsters to be part of the solution to community problems, we can help them learn to respect themselves, and to develop the courage it takes to accept challenges rather than ignoring them.

General Colin Powell discusses this eloquently: "Young people—like adults—usually find that when they make a real effort on behalf of others, they get back more than they contribute." In an article entitled "Everybody's Children," Powell concludes, "Giving to our youth, and helping them learn the joys of giving back, could literally transform America, if we are willing to involve ourselves in the effort."[1]

SOURCE NOTES

We want to thank storyteller Bev Twillmann for her creative input as we developed this tale. The story is related to Motifs K606 *Escape by singing a song. Captive gradually moves away and finally escapes;* K555.2 *Respite from death gained by long-drawn out song;* and K606.2 *Groundhog escapes by persuading captors to dance. Wolves sing and dance; groundhog edges nearer hole and escapes.*

Variants include:

"The Lion on the Path," in Anne Pellowski, *The Story Vine: A Source Book of Unusual and Easy-to-Tell Stories from Around the World* (Macmillan, 1984).

Hugh Tracey, *The Lion on the Path and Other Stories* (Routledge & Kegan Paul, 1967).

"Groundhog Dance," in Margaret Read MacDonald, *Twenty Tellable Tales: Audience Participation Folktales for the Beginning Storyteller* (Wilson, 1986).

The Secret Heart of the Tree

AS TOLD BY ALLAN DAVIES, AN ENGLISHMAN LIVING IN
BLACKRIDGE, WEST LOTHIAN, SCOTLAND.

---

*This light-hearted African tale carries a powerful message
of respect for nature, respect for others, respect for one's word
and honor.*

It was a hot, hot, hot day and Hare was really suffering. Sweat ran off the ends of his ears, and he was panting.

"I need some shade," he said to himself. "If I don't cool down, I'm going to melt." So he hopped (slowly) over to the Baobab tree. It cast a big pool of lovely, cool shade all around its trunk. It looked really good to Hare, but he was a polite creature, so rather than just hopping into the shade, he said to the Baobab tree:

"Baobab, can I rest in your shade, please? It's very hot out here." The Baobab rustled its leaves in surprise and said to Hare, "Of course you can. Stay as long as you like."

Hare hopped into the shade beneath the tree and sat down. It was sooo lovely and cool. A little breeze sprang up from nowhere and ruffled his fur . . . He lay down, stretched out his legs, and felt much, much better.

"Thank you, Baobab. This is a beautiful cool patch of shade you have here. I feel much better already."

The Baobab rustled its leaves, and a ripe, succulent fruit fell out of its branches and landed right next to Hare. Hare ate the fruit slowly, enjoying the juices and sweet taste.

"Thank you, Baobab. How did you know I was thirsty as well?" said Hare. He just lay there for a while, enjoying the peace and quiet, but then he started to itch. Right in the middle of his back, right in the part you just can't reach yourself, no matter how hard you try . . . and you know what that's like. It can easily drive you crazy.

"Baobab, I've got this dreadful itch," he said. "Could I possibly scratch myself against your bark?"

The leaves rustled and the Baobab replied, "Scratch away, Friend."

So Hare had a really good scratch, rubbing his back up and down the Baobab's rough bark . . . It really hit the spot . . . ummmmm . . . goood.

"Thank you, Baobab," he said. "You make a wonderful scratching post."

Leaves rustled and the Baobab said, "You're the first person that's had the courtesy to say please and thank you, so I'd like to show you something in return. I will open up, so you can come inside me, but you must promise not to take anything."

"That would be wonderful," said Hare. " I promise to be careful, and not to take anything."

A small crack started in the top of the Baobab's trunk, then grew wider as it ran down the trunk, all the way to the ground. Then the two halves of the trunk slowly creaked open like two giant doors.

Hare poked his nose inside . . . and then his jaw dropped so far that he nearly tripped over it . . . He hopped further in, over lush green grass. There was a little stream running through a meadow, and a soft, golden light that seemed to come from everywhere at once. He went further in and saw heaped piles of every kind of fruit, ripe and luscious . . . He was still hungry, and went towards them, but then he stopped, remembering his promise.

Then he saw something sparkling in the grass. A carpet of jewels, gold and silver, spread as far as he could see. He picked up a big ruby to look at it, then carefully put it back down, exactly where he had picked it up.

Shaking his head in amazement, Hare went on, deeper and deeper into the heart of the tree. Then he saw a pulsing green light. As he got closer, he saw that the light was coming from an emerald as big as his head, sitting on top of a rock. It was the most beautiful thing that Hare had ever seen, and he reached out towards it longingly . . . then stopped.

"I can see you are someone that keeps your promises," said the Baobab. "Please choose something to take with you, as my gift."

What to take?

Hare thought about the fruit, and how he was still hungry. But if he took a fruit, he'd eat it, and then it would be gone. He went back to the jewels, and after a lot of searching, found a very plain gold ring. He held the ring up.

"Could I possibly take this?" he asked. "It would make a lovely present for my wife."

"Take it, and my blessings with it," replied the Baobab.

And so Hare hurried back out, and the trunk of the tree closed up again. Hare scurried home to his wife—who was absolutely delighted with her present. She put the ring round her tail, and sashayed about looking over her shoulder.

Hare made her promise not to tell anybody where she got the ring, and she agreed. Later on that day, she was hopping out, round and about, when she heard a snicker in her ear. It was Mrs. Hyena.

"Hee . . . hee . . . hee . . . nice ring there, nice ring . . . Where'd ya geddit?"

At first Mrs. Hare wouldn't tell, but Mrs. Hyena was big, and strong, and very mean, and she wouldn't let Mrs. Hare go until she'd got the truth out of her.

That night, when Hyena got home, his wife told him about Mrs. Hare's new jewelry.

"So? Whadd'ya saying here?" said Hyena.

"I'm saying if that stoopid Hare can get a ring, you can get the whole shooting match for me. Hee-hee-hee-hee. So get up off your behind tomorrow and go on down to the Baobab tree, hee-hee-hee . . ."

So, the next morning, Hyena loped down to the Baobab tree.

"Hyah, bub, howya doin? Okay if I grab some shade, pal?"

The tree rustled its leaves and said, "Yes, of course, be my guest."

Hyena sat down and picked his nose for a while. Then he said, "Hey, I'm starving here! Where's the fruit?"

The tree rustled its leaves, said nothing, but dropped a fruit. Hyena scarfed it up in no time, belched, then said, "Got me an itch. Okay to scratch? I mean, I wouldn't want to offend anybody, or nothin'."

"Don't let me stop you," said the tree. So Hyena, who was always itching, had himself a good scratch on the tree's trunk. Then he lay about for a bit, giggling quietly to himself.

"Hey, I done the shade, I done the fruit, I done the scratch . . . When do I get to see inside, hey-ho-ho-ho-ho-ho?"

"Well," said the tree, "if you want, I suppose there's no harm. But you must . . ."

"Yeah, I know, keep the mitts off. I know the score," said Hyena.

The crack appeared in the top of the tree and spread to the ground, and once more the Baobab tree opened wide its secret heart. Hyena bounded inside, looking all over the place.

"Hey, cooooool . . . old Hare was right . . . well, I'll be . . ." He pulled some sacks out of his pocket, scooped up all the fruit, and put them in one sack. The jewels and gold went into another sack. Then Hyena saw the green glow and loped over.

"Cooooool." He didn't think twice, but grabbed the emerald and turned to leave.

But the light in the tree was dying, and the gap in the trunk closing. Hyena ran as fast as he could towards the narrowing strip of daylight.

But he wasn't fast enough. With an almighty crash the trunk slammed shut.

And, as far as I know, he's still in there.

Hyena was the last creature to see the secret heart of a tree. They won't let us in anymore because they don't trust anybody. And who can blame them?

Maybe, one day, we might be lucky enough to win back that trust and see the wonders in the heart of the tree.

Story Notes

When we came across this story posted on Storytell, we immediately fell in love with it! We're very grateful to Allan Davies for generously allowing us to include his breezy retelling in our collection.

Allan says: "I often change the type of tree, to make the tale more accessible. It can work very well if you are standing in front of a particularly impressive specimen of a native tree species—I don't generally say that it was this particular tree, just leave it open for people to make their own minds up.

"I also thought a bit of information about Baobab trees might be of interest:

"They are common throughout much of Africa, and are also known as 'Bottle Trees' or 'Up-side Down Trees.' When in their youth, they look like any other tree, but as they grow older the trunk tends to swell out, sometimes to an enormous degree, so that they look like squat bottles. They can live to a pretty considerable age, and, as they get older, they tend to produce fewer and fewer leaves. Eventually, it can look as though the branches are in fact the roots, and that the tree is somehow growing upside down."

In discussing this story with Allan, we learned that he frequently tells it outdoors, in parks and nature preserves, and often last because it "tends to leave people thoughtful." He has found that the tale is powerful enough to stand on its own, without any need to point up the moral. We agree.

It's not always necessary—or wise—to belabor the message of a story. The power of storytelling lies in its ability to sneak past the conscious mind and into the very heart and soul of people—listeners who recognize and process the messages in their own ways and at their own pace.

Still, as we process this story, some questions naturally arise—as in "which came first, the chicken or the egg?":

Do you have to respect others in order to be able to respect yourself?
Do you have to respect yourself in order to respect others?
Can you respect yourself if you don't respect others?
Can you be respected if you do not show respect?
Can you respect yourself if you don't respect the environment?

We contend that self-respect is a product of respecting others as well as the environment. In order to feel good about yourself, you must treat others as you wish to be treated. And you must treat other living things with that same respect.

We therefore suggest a follow-up activity other than a discussion or an exercise. Take a walk in nature and look for ways to show respect for the environment. Ask children to show respect for Mother Nature (and for themselves and their community) by picking up litter as they go. As a long-term project, the class might adopt a stretch of highway to keep litter-free, or pledge to stage a cleanup at a local park.

By providing an opportunity to act upon the story's message, rather than simply talking about it, you will give children a chance to share in Hare's experience. They will show respect for the earth by keeping it clean, respect for themselves by keeping a pledge, and respect for others by creating a safe, beautiful environment for all living things.

More than anything, this story reveals to us the awesome power of nature, both to give abundantly, as the tree did to respectful Hare, and to destroy, as it did to disrespectful Hyena. For those who plunder the earth without regard to natural habitats or whole ecosystems, it suggests there is a payback.

SOURCE NOTES

Allan Davies heard this story from Pomme Clayton (The Company of Storytellers), who told him it comes from the savanna regions of Africa. Neither he nor we have been successful in locating any print sources.

This is one of many tales about just rewards for good and bad behavior. There are several related motifs: D1556 *Self-opening tree trunk;* Q.2 *Kind and unkind girls;* J2415 *Foolish imitation of lucky man;* and Q41 *Politeness rewarded.*

Bibi and the Singing Drum

Some people learn lessons the hard way. In this story from Zanzibar, two older sisters learn the importance of responsibility, courage, resourcefulness, and persistence when their carelessness results in disaster.

Once there were three sisters who lived with their parents on the island of Zanzibar, East Africa. The oldest sister, Poko, was eleven. Moya was nine. And Bibi, their baby sister, was only six.

One morning, Poko and Moya went to their mother and asked, "Mom, may we go to the beach to spend the morning?"

Mom replied, "Yes, you may go, but you must take your baby sister with you."

Poko started whining right away. "Ah, Mom, why do we have to take that little kindergarten baby with us? She's too little and she walks too slowly. Let us go to the beach by ourselves. Pleeeeaase?"

Mother heard her, but she said, "Now you listen and you listen well. If you do not take your little sister with you to the beach, you will not go at all. Now, what are you going to do?"

With that choice, the two older girls reluctantly took their little sister and set off for the beach. As they had predicted, Bibi lagged behind.

"Come on, you little brat!" shouted the oldest sister.

But Bibi shot back, "I don't care if you're mad. Be mad until you get glad. Mom said I could go, so there!" The sisters knew she was right, but it didn't make them glad. They trudged on through the forest.

Bibi had never been through the forest that led to the beach before. As she followed behind her two older sisters, she heard all the wild birds singing their morning song. It was a beautiful rhapsody which fascinated Bibi and made her gaze in wonderment at the trees. It also slowed her down, which infuriated her older sisters.

But finally, the three girls arrived at the beach. The Indian Ocean stretched out in all its splendor, waves lapping the shore.

The two older sisters, who knew how to swim, went running full-speed into the water, stroking their arms strongly as they went against the ocean waves. Bibi had never been swimming in the ocean before, only wading in the small pond near their village. She stood watching her sisters playing in the water and wished she could join them. Step by step she crept closer to the water's edge, when, SPLASH! a wave came crashing to shore!

"Yikes!" Bibi yelped as she jumped back. But it happened again, SPLASH! "Yikes!"

"Jump back, Honey, jump back!" Moya giggled as she watched Bibi being chased back by the ocean. But the third time, the wave lobbed a seashell onto the sand right at Bibi's feet.

"Yikes . . . ohhhh!" Bibi stood staring at the beautiful gift dropped at her feet by the great wave. She picked up the seashell and examined it carefully. It was white and knobby on the outside, but the inside was smooth and pink and shiny. Bibi ran her fingers all over the shell, then held it to her cheek to feel the satiny coolness of the smooth pink curve.

"Shhhhaaaaaash," said the shell. Bibi nearly dropped the shell in surprise! She could actually hear the sound of the ocean inside. "Shhhhaaaaaash."

"Ohhhh! A beautiful seashell, and it's all mine! I know what—I'll make up a song for my seashell." She held the shell close to her ear, and thought for a moment. Then she began to sing:

> I have a seashell from the sea.
> I have a seashell *just for me!*
> It sounds like the ocean for me to hear.
> It sounds like the ocean in *my* ear.

She sang her song over and over again to be sure she would remember it. Then she put the seashell beside a large rock and began building sand castles.

At noon, the older girls came out of the water and told Bibi it was time to go home. They had walked about ten minutes when Bibi stopped suddenly. "Ohhhh, I forgot my seashell. We have to go back and get it!"

"Go back? For a dumb shell? We're not going back all that way for a dumb seashell, Bibi. We'll get it when we come next week," said Poko.

"No, I don't want to wait till next week," pouted Bibi. " Somebody might take it by then. I want to go get it now!"

"Well, we're not going with you now. If you want it, you have to go back by yourself and get it." And the two older girls turned their backs on Bibi and walked away. They let their little baby sister walk back by herself.

As Bibi walked alone through the forest, she began to be scared. The sounds of the birds and the insects didn't seem so friendly any more. And the thick leaves made dark pools of shadow that reminded her of the darkness under her bed. So she wrapped her arms tightly around herself and began to sing her shell song for comfort:

"I have a seashell from the sea . . . "

Bibi sang her song three times, and she finally reached the beach. When she stepped out of the shade of the trees and onto the sand, she saw the rock—and she saw the shell—but there, right on that same rock, sat a horrible ogre. He had a huge head shaped like a light bulb with one hair on top blowing in the breeze. He had two large bubble eyes that hung out of the sockets like two oranges, and a long witch's nose that curved down towards his chin. His mouth was filled with gaping canine teeth, and when he opened it to speak, green slobber ran out the corners. His long skinny arms hung down off the sides of the rock and ended in long, sharp, yellow nails, and in one of those arms he cradled a conga drum.

Bibi stopped singing, and she stopped walking, and she started to back away from the ogre. But he called out to her in a rusty voice, "What a sweet sounding little song. Who are you?"

"I'm Bibi, and I just want to get my seashell there by the rock."

"Sing that song for me once again, and I'll give you your seashell," croaked the ogre. Bibi really wanted her seashell, so she began to sing.

"I have a seashell from the sea . . ."

"Oh, your voice is much too soft, and I can't hear you too well. Come closer, little girl, come closer."

"I have a seashell . . ."

"Come closer, little girl, come closer."

"I have . . ."

Suddenly, the ogre leaped from the rock and grabbed Bibi. He pulled the drum head from his conga drum, put Bibi inside, threw the seashell on top, and fastened the drum head tightly.

"Now," he chuckled, "I have the only singing drum in the world, and every time I play it, you must sing that song. People will think I have a magic drum, and everywhere I go they will give me food and money and great honor! I shall be rich! But mind, little girl! If you do not sing, you shall not eat."

At that, the ogre took the drum by the strap, swung it over his back like a bookbag, and walked into the forest with it. When he came to a nearby village, he took the drum from his shoulder and shouted, "I have a drum that can sing a song of a seashell! Feed me a meal, and I will have my drum sing for you!"

The people in the village had never heard a singing drum before, so they rushed around to get the ogre some food. After a sumptuous meal, he played the drum and Bibi sang her song.

Meanwhile, the sisters had just gotten back home for lunch. They came skipping into the house calling, "Hi, Mom, we're home for lunch!"

Mother looked at them, and behind them, then back at her two daughters. "Where is Bibi?"

Poko said, "Who?"

Mother gave her a hard look. "That little girl you've been living with for six years, that's who. Where is your baby sister?"

The girls looked at each other. "You tell her."

"I'm not going to tell her! You tell her."

"Tell me what?" demanded their mother.

The girls looked at their toes as they explained, "She said she had to go back to the beach for a dumb seashell, so we told her if she wanted to do that, she could just go by herself."

"What? You let that little girl go back through the forest by herself? Go get my baby out of those woods right now!"

The two girls flew down the path and back through the forest, expecting to see Bibi any minute. But they reached the beach without seeing any sign of her. Panicking now, they ran back home and told their parents the bad news.

A search party was formed, and all the men of the village looked for Bibi. But after seven days and seven nights, they finally had to give up the search. Her sisters didn't give up, though, and every day they went into the forest calling her name.

Meanwhile, the ogre continued to take the drum from village to village, tricking people into thinking he had a singing drum, until one day he came to the village where Bibi's family lived. He went to the center of the village, and shouted out, "I have drum that can sing a song! Feed me a meal and I will have my drum sing for you!"

The people brought food and gathered round as the man played the drum and Baby Sister sang:

> I have a seashell from the sea.
> I have a seashell *just for me*.
> It sounds the ocean for me to hear.
> It sounds like the ocean in *my* ear.

Among the people gathered around the drum were Poko and Moya. As they listened to the singing, their eyes grew wide. "That's Bibi's voice!" whispered Moya. "And that's Bibi's song!" whispered Poko. "We have to get her out of the drum." Quickly, the two sisters came up with a plan. They went back to the ogre.

"Please, sir, would you mind taking the bucket to the river to get us some fresh water? It's getting too dark for us to go the river alone, and we want to make a special stew for you."

The ogre was reluctant to go, but the girls pleaded and begged, and he finally left with the bucket. As soon as he was out of sight, they unfastened the drumhead and found Bibi crouched inside, holding tightly to her seashell. They helped her out of the drum, hugged her hard, and hid her in the bushes. Then they raced to a nearby tree and took down a hornet's nest, lowered it carefully inside the drum, and fastened the head back on the drum.

They were just in time. The ogre returned with the water bucket, demanding that they prepare the stew that they had promised.

"We will be happy to make the stew. Would you play your singing drum for us as we work?"

"Certainly I will play my magic drum," he replied proudly. He sat down and began to play. All of the villagers gathered to hear the singing again, but all they heard was the normal pats and raps of the conga drum. The people began to grumble, "That's not singing. What happened to your magic drum?"

The man pounded harder and whispered to the drum, "Sing, little girl, or you'll go hungry!" But still, no song came from the drum.

"What's the matter, does your drum have laryngitis?" "Cat got it's tongue?" "Is it shy?" The people began to heckle the man, and he played harder and louder. And as he pounded away, the hornets inside got madder and madder.

Finally, he began to hear a loud humming coming from inside the drum. He leaned closer to listen, but he couldn't figure out what the sound was.

"Excuse me, Ladies and Gentlemen. I need to adjust the head of my drum so that the song can come out." He turned his back and bent over the drum, unfastening the drumhead to peek inside. As he did, the angry hornets came buzzing out, and aimed for the first target they could find—the strange man's ugly face!

"YEOOOOOW! Ow! Ow! OWWWWWWW!" the man reeled away from the drum and out of the village, galloping into the forest with the angry hornets in full pursuit.

The people of the village laughed and laughed as watched. But then their laughter turned to tears of joy as Poko and Moya led their little sister out of the bushes and into their parents' arms.

That night and for many nights afterward, Poko and Moya told the whole village the story of how they had recognized Bibi's voice inside the drum, and the trick they had played on the strange man. And that night and for many nights afterward, the people praised the two sisters for their quick thinking and courageous actions.

But Poko and Moya never forgot that it was their carelessness in letting Bibi go back into the forest alone that caused all the trouble. They never forgot the fear and the anguish of losing her. And they never let anything happen to her again.

STORY NOTES

Here is a story for all ages. Primary-school children of Bibi's age identify with her longing to go to the beach, her determination to retrieve her shell, and her fear of the dark forest and the loathsome ogre. Older children identify whole-heartedly with Poko and Moya in their desire to be unfettered by a pesky younger sibling and her silly obsession with shells, and in their panic and anguish of finding they had put her in danger. And adults identify with the mother in her insistence on sending Bibi to the beach with her older sisters, her grief in Bibi's loss, and her joy at her daughter's safe return.

The tale provokes laughter, fear, suspense, and joy. It also provokes lively discussions about responsibility, courage, resourcefulness, and persistence. One successful approach that we have used in discussing this story is character analysis.

"Bibi and the Singing Drum" introduces us to new people, and gives us the opportunity to watch them relate to others. As Jean Grasso Fitzpatrick discusses in *Once Upon a Family*, stories help children live in a "real world" of paradoxes.[1] Even in this short tale, the characters present those paradoxes, being willful, irresponsible, and disobedient in the beginning of the story, then becoming respectful and courageous by the end.

After the story, ask the children to list "good" character traits such as honesty, respect, and responsibility on the board, along with their opposites ("bad" character traits). This will serve as a ready reference for the exercise. Now put each character's name on the board (or, in smaller groups, on a piece of paper).

Which traits does each character exhibit? As the students list the qualities, ask, "How do we know this about the character?

> By what the character says?
> By what the character does?
> By what others say and do about this character?"

After the students are satisfied that the lists are complete, use some of these questions as discussion starters:

- Who was your favorite character in the story and why?
- Was this character a "good guy" or a "bad guy"?
- Why do you judge him or her "good" or "bad"?
- Do the characters change in the story? Do they learn anything? If so, what?
- Did the "bad guys" get punished for wrongdoing?
- Did the "good guys" get rewarded?
- Do you think the story was "fair"—that is, did the characters "get what they deserved" in the end?

We also discuss what the intentions of the character were, and how these intentions affect our opinion of a character. Did the sisters *intend* for harm to come to Bibi or were they simply inattentive? *Intent* to harm would have been malicious, but carelessness, while it had the same results, isn't evil.

You might want to try some role-playing with this story, asking two children to be the older siblings, and someone to be Bibi, who has just learned she gets to go the beach for the first time. Ask the actors to play the scene in several ways: (1) as it developed in the story, (2) an even worse scenario, and (3) the best-case scenario. Does any character's behavior stay the same in all three scenes? How can Bibi's behavior affect her sisters' response? How can one older sister affect another's response? Does the *intent* of the characters change?

This exercise helps children recognize that "good" and "bad" come in many degrees, from the "bad" behavior of a naughty little girl to the evil behavior of an ogre. It also helps children recognize that every decision carries with it the opportunity to make good and bad choices. All the sisters made bad choices early in the story, but they learned from their mistakes and made responsible and resourceful choices at the end.

SOURCE NOTES

This is one of the first stories that we discovered we both had in our repertoires—but we told it with different endings. The original source for both of us was Verna Aardema's *Bimwili and the Zimwi: a Tale from Zanzibar* (Dial, 1985).

Motif G422.1.1 *Girl put into drum and forced to sing.*

Other versions are:

Anne Rockwell, *When the Drum Sang: An African Folktale* (Parent's Press, 1970). Bantu variant.

Kathleen Arnott, *African Myths and Legends* (Walck, 1962). Bantu variant.

Ricardo Alegria, *Wishes: a Collection of Puerto Rican Folktales* (Harcourt, Brace, World, 1969). Puerto Rican variant.

Teen Rap Crisis

BY DEANDRE REDD, PERFORMED ON CASSETTE AND CD
BY BOBBY NORFOLK AND KEITH TORREY ON
STORYTELLER IN A GROOVE (EARWIG, 1992).

Studies indicate that one of the main factors contributing to teen suicide, pregnancy, gang involvement, drug and alcohol use, and giving in to peer pressure is low self-esteem. This up-beat hip-hop story written by a teenager in St. Louis, Missouri, speaks to these issues in a voice that kids understand.

Read and perform this piece in "hip-hop rap" beat, putting the emphasis on the fourth beat of the line. It takes some practice to get it right—listen to the tape to get the rhythm if you're having trouble!

Teen crusader:

This is a story all teens might know
About the path to choose and the way to go.
Now José is gonna talk about those who tried
Living life on the edge, committing suicide.

José:

Hey, my name is José, and I'm telling you, Friend,
Suicide ain't how you want it to end.
Overdose on pills, shoot yourself in the head.

But then you realize you don't wanna be dead.
So what, you got an F: try a little harder.
Accomplish your dreams and soon you'll go farther.
Jumping off a cliff ain't gonna make it better.
Have a talk with yourself, and write yourself a long letter.
Pick-ups and knock-downs happen every day.
Don't let those two stand in your way.
Life will go on, and you'll soon find out
That suicide isn't what it's about.
Heed my advice, cause you see I've tried.
Who told you life ain't worth living?
'Cause, Boy, they lied.
So take it from me, cause, Homeboy, I should know.
Take your time, think it over, and live life slow.

Teen crusader:

So now I'm talking 'bout teenage sex,
About the dos and the don'ts
And a girl named Beth.

Beth:

Hi! My name is Beth. Don't be in a rush,
'Cause when it comes to sex, some boys you can't trust.
First, he's lovey-dovey, and wants to get together.
When you tell him the news, he'll say he's heard better.
When I said I might get pregnant, he said, "I don't care."
But now that I am, he said, "Man, it ain't fair!"
So make the right move, before your mom's on your case.
'Cause you shouldn't have gotten pregnant, in the first place.
Check this! Life is fun if you live as a teen.
Now I'm living as a grown-up, if you know what I mean.
Live your life, but it's yours to choose.
So instead of buying diapers, and baby shoes,
Stay out of sex, for now you really shouldn't do it.

Set a goal for life and be sure to pursue it.

The way it happened for me was just like in a movie,

Except the "happy ending" didn't feel so groovy.

My "happy ending" makes me wanna cry.

'Cause the boy who got me pregnant ain't got a B-A-B-Y.

So leave it alone cause you really shouldn't bother,

'Cause the boy who got me pregnant didn't want to be a father.

Teen crusader:

Hold up for a second, the story ain't complete.

L.G.A. is gonna tell you 'bout gangs in the street.

L.G.A.

Yo! My name is L.G.A., but you can call me "L."

Sit back for a while, I got a story to tell.

One day I was chillin' on Main and 5th,

I was waiting on my boy to come and give me a lift.

When I saw so many dudes they could've made a team,

I said, "I know they want to fight me," so I started to scream.

But I said, "No let me keep my cool,"

"Besides, screaming out loud makes me feel like a fool."

When the leader came up, I started to laugh.

He said, "What's funny, Home B? I want everything you have."

I said, "You want my chains and all my money?"

For some strange reason, I didn't find that funny.

He said, "That's right, boyee, I want your money and chains.

If I don't get it fast, I'm gonna bust your brain."

Right about then, he pulled out a knife,

So I gave it all because of fear for my life.

When I got home, and told my mom what went on,

She said, "I'm calling the police," and she picked up the phone.

They arrested the boy and we went downtown,

So I told the police what went down.

I told 'em 'bout the money, the knife and the chain.

He said, "The thugs today, why they must be insane."
The boy went to jail and did his time.
Well, that's very much the purpose of me saying this rhyme.
See, 'cause when the boy got out, his urge for crime never chilled.
Later on that year, the young boy was killed.
Well, the story is told, and I'm going to go home.
By the way, L.G.A. stands for Leave Gangs Alone.

Teen crusader:

Well, I'm back again and by now you see
That you can live your life how you want it to be.
Next on the agenda is a girl named Suzie.

Suzie:

I was at a party five years ago.
Back then they used to call cocaine "snow."
My friend walked up, around a quarter to nine.
She said, "Yo, Sue, let's do a couple of lines."
Little did I know she meant a couple of lines of coke.
When I found out, I said, "You must be a joke."
We argued to nine, then I said, "Enough."
"I might as well go and do the stuff."
So, of course, I did and it felt good.
So I did it again, like any average person would.
I did it over and over, again and again.
Little did I know that coke was frying my brain.
I was a slave, and coke was my master.
I was on a train, headed for disaster.
Sooner or later, I knew that I'd die.
But I said, "I don't care, just as long as I'm high."
My mom found out, and it broke her heart.
She tried to get me off coke, while the family fell apart.
I loved my mom, and she loved me.
But I didn't seem to love her more than C-O-K-E.

To lie and cheat is one thing, to steal is another.
But I had to draw the line when I couldn't respect my mother.
This drug was on my back, and I was going crazy.
I have to leave it alone or I'll be pushing up daisies.
I had to get some help to help the situation,
So I went to the clinic to get rehabilitation.
Now I'm better, and I'm through with those days.
The drugs are still there, but I've changed my ways.
The move to make it the one that's right.
And long as I live, I'll regret that night.
The girl who got me started became a slave,
So I hope she took her master with her to the grave.
The drug is addicting, so if you don't try,
You won't have to use coke as an excuse when you die.
My story is told, and every part is true.
All I can say is, "Don't let it happen to YOU."

Teen crusader:

So I guess you know the right move to make,
Especially when it's your life at stake.
My boy Dave is the smartest of us all.
But when it came to peer pressure, he had a great fall.

Dave:

Hello! My name is Dave and all I can say,
Is there's a real big problem with peer pressure today.
I was the one who always got As,
And felt inside my heart that education pays.
Where the story goes wrong is when I didn't feel cool,
And everyone called me the nerd of the school.
No one talked to me: that made me feel bad.
I sat down for awhile and had a talk with my dad.
He said, "Son, don't you worry; you're smarter than a few.
It doesn't worry me; don't let it worry you."

He said, "In fact, my son, you should really feel proud.
"Don't always be like the rest of the crowd."
Well, I took his advice and didn't worry, you see.
'Cause in the long run, I'm responsible for me.
When others who are smart want to be cool,
And go along with the crowd, they're really some fools.
I'm intelligent and I'm proud to say,
An education is the only way.
As hard as it is to prepare for a career—
Forget peer pressure and put your brain in gear.
Believe, I know being different is hard.
But to succeed in life, you have to do your part.
Most people get together and straighten their heads.
Those who don't, it's a shame, it's often said
By parents of children who want to be cool,
"He could've been a success if he'd only stayed in school."
Peer Pressure is life you experience, my friend.
Only you can be the judge of how you want it to end.
Well, if you make the right move, then you'll feel better.
Instead of being cool, be a goal setter!

Teen crusader:

Last on the list is the worst of all:
Teens getting addicted to alcohol.
At parties, you may think it is a casual high:
Easy to get and not hard to buy.
But if you keep drinking, you'll see in the end
That alcohol is not a casual friend.
You drink some at home and some at school
So you'll think that they think that you're really cool.
I remember a friend that I once had.
He got addicted to drinking because of his dad.
Why his father didn't care is beyond my knowledge.
If my friend was alive, he would've entered college.

But he isn't. Though you still have to be brave,
My friend took his problem with him to the grave.
Leave drinking alone, for now and for good.
I know some poor mothers who are wishing you would.
My friend started drinking and had no chance of surviving—
Killed himself and many others because of drunk driving.
My friend is gone and I miss him so bad.
He might still be here if it wasn't for his dad.
So, you see, I'm not perfect, far from it, my friend—
But you see old age is the best way to end.
I'm going to party 'till I drop and I'm not going to move.
I'm not drinking 'cause I'm thinking that life is going to improve.
Don't drink at parties 'cause the drinks are there.
Alcohol will take a victim and it doesn't care.
Yes, it gets its victim most every day.
If you don't think about drinking, then drinking will stay
In a place, on a corner, where someone will buy
A real cheap high and an easy way to die.
You're a keen teen, you don't have the ability
To live a grownup life, with adult responsibilities.
The stories that were told were real-life problems.
The choices are yours. Maybe you can help solve them.
These stories were told by the Teen Crusader—
I'm gone for now, but I hope to see ya later.

STORY NOTES

Hip-hop or rap-style music seems to be somehow encoded in the
genetics of today's youth, regardless of color or economic status.
Taking that concept further, DeAndre Redd's powerful piece is the
total answer to "gangsta rap" and its negative implications. Coming
180 degrees, dispensing positive survival messages throughout, this
poem drives home those values parents desperately want instilled in
their children.

During a residency at Alaska Children's Services, a residential treatment center for youth with severe behavioral and emotional disorders, Bobby shared "Teen Rap Crisis" with all the groups, choosing one or two segments per session and following up with serious discussion about the messages and the content. The teens, most of whom had first-hand experience with one or more of the problems described in the poem, were enthralled with the piece, and immediately clamored to learn and perform it themselves.

This was successfully accomplished—even the nonreaders and poor readers in the group were able to learn the words through repetition and intense motivation. We provided printed copies of the words, a copy of the tape, and plenty of practice time. In a couple of weeks, these kids were able to send a positive message very powerfully: from the heart.

Armed with "Teen Rap Crisis," many of the young people announced plans to share their struggles and subsequent progress with others when they returned to their schools and communities. While most of them would not have been comfortable in "witnessing" about their problems in conventional ways, the medium of rap allowed them to feel at ease, and may help them to turn others away from trouble before it begins.

SOURCE NOTES:

DeAndre Redd notes: "I wrote Teen Rap Crisis to make teens aware of the problems going on in today's society as far as peer pressure, gang involvement, alcohol and drug use, teenage pregnancy, and teen suicide. I want to help solve these problems. Listen to this rap and hopefully, it will help you to face and solve yours."

This rap was DeAndre's first published composition. It won an award in a teen writing contest at Dignity House in St. Louis, Missouri, where it was publicly performed. Ponchita Argeard was the sponsor and director of the project.

Kantchil Waits for the World to End

Kantchil the Mouse Deer is Borneo's equivalent to Anansi: small, clever, and full of mischief. In this tale, she uses patience and ingenuity to get out of trouble she has "fallen into" (pardon the pun).

One day, Kantchil was running as fast as the wind through the forest, having a contest with herself to see if she could get home even more quickly than the day before. She was running so fast that the wind made her eyes water, and she couldn't see properly where she was going.

But Kantchil wasn't worried—she ran on these paths every day, and she was sure that she knew them blindfolded.

But she was wrong! Suddenly, Kantchil felt herself falling, falling, falling into a deep, wide hole! She landed with a thud.

"Yow!"

As she rubbed her bruises, Kantchil appraised her situation. The hole was very, very deep, with straight, slippery walls, and there was nothing in the pit except a huge, green banana leaf.

Experimentally, she jumped a few times, but gave that up as soon as she was sure that she could never jump high enough to get out. She tried a bit of climbing, but she couldn't get a grasp on the smooth, slippery sides of the hole.

"Hmmmmm."

Now, Kantchil knew she had to get out of there. But she also knew that jumping up and down and slipping and sliding and wearing herself out wouldn't help. She felt bruised and sore, but she knew that crying wouldn't help, either. And she was hungry—but there was no one to complain to. So Kantchil sat down to wait—and think.

After awhile, she heard rustling in the undergrowth above her head, then the light was suddenly blocked by a big, fat head. Kantchil recognized the silhouette of Boar, the wild pig. She quietly picked up the banana leaf, and studied it intently.

"Hey, Kantchil! Whaddaya doing in that hole?" Boar grunted.

Kantchil didn't answer, but only kept studying the leaf.

"Hey, Kantchil! I said, Whaddaya doing in that hole?"

Kantchil acted startled. She looked up at Boar with her eyes wide.

"Oh, Boar, I'm waiting for the end of the world," she whispered.

"Huh? End of what?"

"The end of the world. See, right here on this Magic Leaf it says,

> Behold the truth upon this leaf,
> Today the world will end in grief.
> To live you must be in the Deep Deep Hole.
> But do not sneeze, or Out You Must Go!
> So it is written.

"Well, then, move over, cause I'm coming in!" grunted Boar, and he jumped right in beside Kantchil.

"I wish you hadn't done that, Boar," said Kantchil sadly. "You know how much you always snuffle and sneeze, because you always have your nose in the dirt. I'll have to throw you out when you sneeze, and you're awfully heavy. You're going to be hard to throw, Boar."

"I won't sneeze, Kantchil. I won't even sniffle. I'll hold my nose—see? Don't worry, you won't be throwing *me* out of this hole. We'll wait for the end of the world together."

So Boar held his nose, and they sat and they waited. Boar grunted. He groaned. He rooted in the earth and he kicked up dirt clods.

"I'm bored with waiting, Kantchil. Nothing's going to happen. Let's get out of here," said Boar through his pinched-up nose.

"Go ahead, Boar, if you're so BORED. You get on out of here. I'm waiting for the end of the world right here in this hole where it's safe."

"Oh, all right, Kantchil. I'll wait here with you. But it sure is BORING!"

Just then the hole grew dark again. Tiger stood above them, laughing and pointing into the hole.

"You two sure do look stupid down there!" he growled.

"You're the one who's stupid, Tiger!" grunted Boar. "We're down here waiting for the end of the world."

"What are you talking about, Boar?" Tiger growled menacingly. "How dare *you* call *me* stupid?"

"I'm talking about the message on Kantchil's Magic Leaf. Read it to him, Kantchil."

"Okay, listen, Tiger:

> Behold the truth upon this leaf,
> Today the world will end in grief.
> To live you must be in the Deep Deep Hole.
> But do not sneeze, or Out You Must Go!
> So it is written.

"I'm coming down!" said Tiger, and he suited actions to words.

"Oh, Tiger, it was silly of you to come down here," said Kantchil. "You're always sneezing, cause you have so many hairballs! We'll have to throw you out before you know it!"

Tiger growled softly. "Don't bet on it, Kantchil. I'll hold my breath—I won't even breathe. Now just hush up, and we'll wait for the end of the world."

Tiger took a deep breath and held it.

The three sat in silence for awhile. But Tiger grew restless. He began to pace 'round and 'round in the tiny space. Boar began to grunt and groan again.

"There's nothing to do in this hole!" Tiger wheezed. "I'm tired of waiting for the end of the world."

"I'm BORED!" Boar said again and again.

Kantchil sat and read the banana leaf and waited.

Suddenly the sunlight disappeared completely. Elephant stood above them, blocking the light.

"Shhh!" whispered Boar. "Don't tell Elephant about the leaf. She's way too big to come down here."

"Hush! That's mean," said Kantchil. "I have to tell her if she asks. It's only fair."

Just then, Elephant trumpeted, "*Hello down there! What do you think you're doing in that hole?*"

"We're waiting for the end of the world, Elephant," Kantchil replied. "Listen to what it says on this Magic Leaf:

Behold the truth upon this leaf,
Today the world will end in grief.
To live you must be in the Deep Deep Hole.
But do not sneeze, or Out You Must Go!
So it is written.

"Oh. Well, then it's lucky for me that I came along. Gang-way!"

The other three squeezed to the sides of the hole as Elephant dropped down. The hole was filled from side to side with animals.

"Oh, Elephant, I wish you had paid more attention. Look, it says, 'But do not sneeze, or Out You Must Go!' Now, Elephant, you know that with that great big nose of yours, you're always sneezing! And you're sooooo heavy. How will we ever throw you out?" Kantchil asked.

"No, Kantchil, you'll see. I'll tie my nose in a knot. I won't sneeze, see?" and Elephant tied her nose in a tight knot.

All the animals wriggled in discomfort, waiting for the world to end. Tiger couldn't pace, so he tapped his toes. Boar grunted and groaned. Elephant began to sway just a bit from side to side.

Bump went Elephant. "Ow!" yelled Boar through his nose.

Bump went Elephant. "Umph!" snarled Tiger, still holding his breath.

Bump went Elephant. "What's that? What's that?" Kantchil cried suddenly. "Somebody's getting ready to sneeze!"

"Well, it's not me!" grunted Boar. "I haven't sniffled or snuffled."

"It's not me!" wheezed Tiger. "I haven't twitched or itched."

"It's not me!" trumpeted Elephant. *"Cause I tied my nose in a knot to make sure I won't sneeze!"*

"Well, *somebody* is getting ready to sneeze!" said Kantchil. "I can feel it in my bones. I can feel it in my skin. I can feel it in my . . . in my . . . in my . . . oh, no! In my *nose*! *I'm* going to sneeze! Ah-ah-ah, ah-ah-ah, ah-ah-AH-CHOO!"

No sooner did Kantchil sneeze than she felt herself being grabbed by three sets of paws. She was thrown high into the air, out of the hole and onto the forest floor.

"Waaaaaaaaahoooooooo!"

"But do not sneeze, or out you must go!" the animals in the hole chanted to Kantchil.

"So it is written," said Boar.

"Yeah, so it is written," wheezed Tiger.

"So it is written," said Elephant.

"Is it so?" asked Kantchil. "Look at the Magic Leaf, and read what is written upon it."

Boar grabbed the leaf and turned it over and over.

"Nothing!" Boar yelled. "It says nothing!"

Tiger stared at the leaf. "It's just a leaf! What's going on?"

Elephant took the leaf. *"It's an ordinary leaf! It's not magic at all, Kantchil!"*

"Oh, yes, it is magic," called Kantchil. "With a little patience, and the help of my good friends, it got me out of that hole in the ground!"

STORY NOTES

We see this story as one about delayed versus instant gratification. Our culture thrives on instant gratification. We have microwaves for instant heat and the Internet for instant communication. But with our instant culture, we also have traffic jams, slow elevators, and long lines. We have to learn to deal with delayed gratification in an instant world.

Most of us respond to this delayed gratification with frustration, irritation, and impatience. Not Kantchil. Surely she wanted out of her uncomfortable situation immediately—she was bruised and hungry. But rather than scream and moan and throw tantrums, she studied her situation, then calmly evaluated her options. She made a plan and waited patiently until the plan came to fruition. While she waited, she probably entertained herself with watching her companions squirm in discomfort at the long wait.

Observe how Kantchil's behavior contrasts with that of Boar, Tiger, and Elephant. Even though Kantchil knew she was in trouble, her patience and calmness allowed her to judge the situation accurately and to problem-solve successfully. Perhaps if Boar, Tiger and Elephant had been less impetuous, they too would have assessed the situation better and not ended up in the hole! (It's always interesting to ask kids how the other animals escaped from the hole after Kantchil ran on home. We purposefully left that to the listeners' problem-solving skills.)

Waiting for the world to end was pretty difficult for everyone but Kantchil. The other animals engaged in useless fidgeting and kvetching, rather than settling down to think and plan for their possible future after that cataclysmic event occurred. There were surely some productive things they could have been doing down in that hole.

As was true for Boar, Elephant, and Tiger, it's the waiting that children have the most trouble with. They have to wait for the bell to ring; wait until the weekend; wait until Daddy gets home; wait until they're older; wait, wait, wait.

And waiting doesn't get too much easier as we grow older, judging from the frustration level of drivers on the highway and folks in long "express" checkout lines. Much of the stress of everyday living comes from waiting.

How can we help children (and ourselves) develop patience?

Several years ago, we came across a Hassidic maxim that, at first reading, sounded like an oxymoron: take joy in the waiting. How can you be joyful while waiting? The very nature of waiting implies that the joy, or the gratification, will come when the waiting is *over*. How, then, can one take joy in the *process* of waiting?

It takes practice. It takes conscious effort. It takes determination and requires vigilance. But it can be done.

Some summers back, I drove an average of one thousand miles a week down endless South Georgia highways. Picture long, straight flat expanses of road that are marked 55 mph, then drop suddenly to 45, then 35, and sometimes (ARGH!) 25, before gradually regaining that grudging 55 mph. Imagine my longing to reach my destination, hungry for any kind of food, eager to stretch and walk and do anything other than sit in that car yet another five hours and drive. Got the picture?

Did I take joy in waiting for that drive to end? Admittedly, I wasn't successful at being joyful every inch of every mile. But I did find a joyful occupation in looking for blossoms along the side of the road. In Georgia, the highway department has seeded thousands of wildflowers along the verges and in the medians of the roads. Not only that, but truly wild wildflowers sprinkle the drainage ditches and fencerows, and cultivated plants grow in populated areas. Once I began to notice all those flowers, I began to take joy in the drive.

Miles melted away as I watched for those flowers. There was rarely a moment when a blossom of some kind or other wasn't visible. Sometimes I had to search to find the dandelion growing beside the shreds of an old tire, but that just made it more interesting.

"Taking joy" takes practice, conscious effort, and vigilance. Time after time, I'd catch myself checking the time against the odometer and against the map, willing the drive to be shorter, and longing to press the pedal to the metal and go a whole lot faster than the law allowed. Time after time, I had to remind myself to look for the flowers, and take joy. Thankfully, taking joy can be habit-forming!

The flower search wasn't just a way to kill time. It was a positive action against boredom, frustration, and impatience. Rather than gazing apathetically through the windshield, I took note with interest, focusing on beauty. It's hard not to smile when you spot a drainage ditch almost choked with golden day lilies, or see the whole median ablaze with poppies.

Take joy in the waiting.

Ask the group to name the kinds of waiting they have to do. Start with the typical short but frustrating waiting situations they find themselves in, then ask for the more long-term waits—waiting to be old enough to drive, or to date, or to vote. List everything in a long column on the board.

Then ask students to describe their typical way of dealing with these waits. Do they complain, moan, groan, watch the clock, and get into mischief? Do they get restless and fidget and pace, and drum on the desk and tap their feet? Do they slip into lethargy? Do they read or study or listen to music? List these responses in another column.

Now, introduce the concept of taking joy in the waiting, and ask people to explain what that means to them. We think it means identifying and focusing on what's good about the situation (the chance to see all those wildflowers) rather than what's bad (the long, long drive). Help them understand that the *process* of reaching a goal can be just as joyful as the goal itself.

Then examine their responses in the "ways of dealing with waiting" column. Which of these could be classified as "taking joy"? Reading a book, listening to music, even daydreaming can be joyful, constructive experiences which lead towards the awaited goal or accomplish another task in the meantime. Using waiting time productively is one form of taking joy in the waiting.

After the responses have been evaluated (a lot of discussion usually takes place before that occurs), ask the group to think of other ways to "take joy." Some situations, such as waiting to be old enough to drive, can be really challenging and require creativity in order to develop strategies for "taking joy." Remind students to identify what might be "good" about the cases they are discussing (not being old enough to drive means not having to pay for insurance, or not having to get up at

5 a.m. to take Dad to the airport). Small group discussions often yield some very insightful possibilities.

As we have mentioned, "taking joy in the waiting" takes practice and conscious effort. For that reason, we suggest journal-keeping as an effective way to make students more aware of the kinds of situations that make them impatient, and the ways in which they deal with these things.

Ask students to keep a journal for one month, noting the kinds of waiting situations they have faced each day, and how they have reacted. Ask them to make special note of the times when they found a way to "take joy." Over the period of a month, most students report an increase in the instance of "joyful" responses, and a corresponding decrease in frustration and impatience.

Source Notes

Motif K652.1 *Kantchil tricks others into pit and gets self thrown out.* Published versions include:

Betty Boegehold, *Small Deer's Magic Tricks* (Coward, McMann & Geoghegan, Inc., 1977).

Harold Courlander, *Kantchil's Lime Pit and Other Stories from Indonesia* (Harcourt, Brace, 1950).

Betsy Maestro and Giulio Maestro, *A Wise Monkey's Tale* (Crown, 1975). (African variant: "If very wise you want to be, come down here, wait, and see.")

Barney McCay

In this Gullah variant of "Hansel and Gretel," Jack and his sister Mary try to out-trick their mother, but learn to respect Mom's wishes for their personal safety and well-being—not to mention her incredible intuition and resourcefulness!

There once was a boy named Jack, and he had a sister named Mary. Now, Jack started an incident that he couldn't get out of, and got his sister Mary to be co-conspirator to the crime.

Do you know what these two kids did? They lied to Moms!

Now, they should've known better: that you cannot out-trick Moms. Mothers have this special power—some call it "Motherwit"; others call it "The Sixth Sense"; some even call it "intuition." Whatever the name, it is a knowledge mothers have of when their kids get hurt or in trouble. There is a stirring inside of Moms that lets her know. Pops has this power, too, but it occasionally needs some fine tuning.

Now, Moms, because of her infinite wisdom with her kids, owned three dogs that saved them from the evil ol' hag. They were called Barney McCay (the lead dog), Doodle de Doo, and Sue-Boy. Even so, the kids had to learn the hard way what my elders used to say to me: "What goes around comes around."

One evening Jack, knowing it was too close to dinnertime and night, got his sister Mary to go in on a lie to their mother.

"Mary, Mary, let's trick Mama!" he said, whispering his plan into Mary's ear, "Whisper, whisper, whisper . . ."

Mary said, "Okay, let's do it, tee hee!"

So Jack and Mary went into the kitchen where Mama was preparing dinner. Jack took over.

"Mama, can we go for a little short walk into the forest? We promise we'll be back before dinnertime."

Now, Mama knew her children. She said, "All right, I'll let you kids go for a *short* walk, but you be back here before night. And be back before dinnertime!"

Then Mama had a thought. She reached into the refrigerator and took out a glass of milk and set it on the table. Then she reached into her apron pocket and took out a kernel of magic corn.

She said, "Jack, I want you to take this kernel of magic corn and put it into your pocket. Now, if you get into trouble out there in the woods, I want you to take this kernel of magic corn and throw it on the ground. As soon as that corn hits the ground, the glass of milk at home will turn red! When that glass of milk turns red, I'll know you two kids are in trouble. I will then go out into the yard and untie my three dogs—Barney McCay, Doodle de Doo, and Sue-Boy—and they'll get the job done! You can believe that!"

Then she reached into her pocket and took out a second kernel of corn and gave it to Mary.

"Now, Mary, you take this kernel of magic corn and put it into your pocket. If you get into *big* trouble, take your kernel of corn and throw it on the ground. As soon as the kernel of corn hits the ground, a big ol' sycamore tree will jump out of the ground. Climb to the top of that tree until my three dogs get there."

So Jack and Mary put the corn into their pockets.

Jack said, "Okay, Mom, thanks! We're sure we won't be needing this magic corn. We'll see you before dinnertime."

Jack and Mary got outside and Jack said, "We tricked the ol' girl! Hee hee hee! Come on, Mary, we're outta here!"

And they walked.

And they walked.

And they walked and they walked and they walked and they walked.

And they walked and they walked and they walked and they walked.

And they were not looking where they were going. Tactical error!

The next thing they knew, the sun went from white to orange to red and sank in the western sky. Big shadows crept over the forest floor and the trails disappeared.

Jack looked around, really panicked, and said, "Mary!"

She said, "What?"

He said, "Guess what?"

She said, "What?"

He said, "We're lost! I want my mama! Whaaaaaa! Mama!"

Mary gave him a whack! "Shut up! Get a grip!"

Jack calmed down. "Thanks, I needed that!"

Mary said, "This is no time to panic, boy! We have to keep cool heads and use the buddy system to get ourselves out of this trouble we got ourselves in."

So Jack and Mary held hands and used the buddy system to get out of the trouble they found themselves in. They walked for about ten minutes into the forest and came upon a clearing where they saw a cottage.

Jack said, "Mary, look! There's a house! Maybe we can get some help there and use the phone to call Mama!"

But little did the kids know . . . that was the house of an evil ol' witch! At that very moment, she was stirring up her big cauldron of stew.

She looked like she was about 197 years old! She had gray skin that hung down from her face like melted wax. Ugh!

She had spiked hair that stood straight up on her head. Pow! Every day was a bad hair day for the ol' girl!

One eye went down one way. Zoop!

And the other eye went Zoop! the other way.

She had a hooked nose that went Bam! way out straight, then Bam! down 45 degrees towards the ground!

She had four teeth in her whole head: two at the top and two at the bottom for ripping flesh from bone.

Inside the stewpot, there were bats' toenails, fish eyeballs, buzzard and rat feet, and about five hundred roach legs. She thought, "All it needs is a little oregano! Hee hee hee!"

Jack swaggered right up to the door and told Mary, "I got this."

He knocked: Bomp-ba-ba-bomp-bomp—Bomp Bomp!

The ol' witch said in her ol' witch's voice, "*Who is it at my door?*"

"Whoa!" Jack jumped backwards. "Mary, did you hear that?"

"Yes, I heard that. It means someone's at home, Fool!"

Jack glared at Mary. "Look, don't start, with me, Girl! I don't mean 'somebody's at home,' Smarty Pants! That's a witch in there!"

Mary gave him a look. "Ohhhh, you're Superboy now—you have x-ray vision and you can see right through the front door!"

Jack glared again. "I don't need no x-ray vision, Smarty Pants! I don't like the way that woman said '*Who is it at my door?*'"

Mary replied, "Now, Jack, we don't know if it's a witch or not. But she has a phone, and we have to call Mama!"

From inside the house, the witch called out again, "*Who is it at my door?*"

Jack stammered like Porky Pig, "B-b-b-b-b-bee—it's Jack and Mary. We're two lost children, and we are trying to find our way home!"

The witch said to herself with glee, "Mmmmmmmm! Plump little children! I will have them for my supper!"

And the ol' girl changed her form: Boomp-boomp-*boomp!* She changed into a nice old lady with a blue flower-print dress, blue hair in a bee-hive hairdo, little granny glasses on her face, black nurse's shoes on her feet, and a walking cane. She hobbled to the door and opened it with a sweet smile on her little-old-lady face.

"Ohhhhh, my poor little lost babies! Come on in! Poor babies!" she cooed in her little-old-lady voice.

Jack and Mary entered the old lady's house, and they had a big meal of stew, corn-on-the-cob, candied yams, and cornbread. When they had finished dinner, the old woman gave them chocolate cake and cold strawberry Koolaid for dessert.

Then she said, "Now, you children must be tired. I want you to go upstairs, turn left, and you'll see twin beds. You take a nap, and I'll phone your mama."

They gave the old woman their number and started upstairs as she pretended to call their mama. But she was just punching numbers at random: beep-beep-beep—beep-beep-beep—beep. And when the voice came on the other end of the line it answered, "Sam's Meat Market!"

She snorted, "Wrong number!" and slammed the phone down, chuckling an evil witchy laugh. *Heh-heh-heh-heh-hehhhhhh!*

Now, Jack still had a bad feeling about that woman, and when he and Mary got upstairs, his intuition kicked in: *Pow!*

Jack looked around and saw a room full of pumpkins. He whispered, "Mary! Just in case that old woman is a witch, let's take these pumpkins out of this room and put them in the room with the twin beds and cover them up. Then we can peek through the crack in the door across the hall and see what happens!"

Well, Mary's intuition was kicking some, too, so she agreed. The two kids took the pumpkins out of the pumpkin room and put them in the twin beds and covered them up. Then they went back across the hall and peeked through the crack in the door.

Meanwhile, downstairs . . . the old woman was busy too. She changed back into the evil ol' witch: Boomp-boomp-*boomp*! She went to the closet and got out her ax and sharpened it up: *Ch-ch-ch-ch-ch-ch-ch-chhhh! Ch-ch-ch-ch-ch-ch-ch-chhhh! Ch-ch-ch-ch-ch-CH-CH!*

Then the ol' witch started up the stairs, ax held high over her head. When she got to the second floor, she crept down the hall, peeking from side to side with the ax still poised overhead. Jack and Mary could see all of this from the crack in the door. They stayed as quiet and still as dust, and watched as the hag reached the bedroom where she thought Jack and Mary were napping.

Sloooowly, she pushed the door open.

Sloooowly, she walked to the beds.

Then, *Thwap!* she threw the covers back!

"Pumpkins!"

Jack and Mary had seen enough. They bolted from that room where they were hiding. They ran down the stairs in a flash and tore out the front door.

The ol' witch was looking for them up and down the hallway. *"Where are those children?"* she shrieked as she ran from room to room, kicking doors open and ripping covers off of beds. Abruptly, she looked out a window and spotted them running into the forest.

"Come back here!" she screeched.

Jack and Mary ran even faster when they heard that.

"Come on, Mary, let's get outta here!" Jack yelled to his sister as they went into overdrive: *booga-de-booga-de-booga-de!*

The ol' witch ran to her broom closet and pulled out her flying broom. She stood up in the window sill, straddled the broom, and flew out the window in hot pursuit.

"Come back here!" she shouted from her broom as she started to close the gap between herself and the kids.

She had lightning bolts in her fingertips! When she flung her hands towards the ground, lightning bolts sprang from her hands: *Boom! Boom!* She hurled one bolt towards the ground, and it ricocheted up and hit Jack right in his little bottom.

"Yeow!" Jack yelled as he grabbed his backside and jumped up and down. "Time to get out Mama's magic corn!" He shoved his hand into his pocket and grabbed the kernel of magic corn Mama had given him and threw it to the ground.

As soon as the corn hit the ground, the glass of milk at home turned red.

Mama was pacing the kitchen floor and muttering in worried-Mama tones, "Where are my children?" All of a sudden, she glanced at the table and saw that the glass of milk had turned red.

"Oh, my goodness!" Both hands went to her face as she stared at that red milk in horror. "My children!"

Mama grabbed a handful of the kids' clothes, ran outside, and untied her three dogs, Barney McCay, Doodle-de-Doo and Sue-Boy. She held the clothes to the dogs' noses: "Here, dogs, smell my kids' clothes. Get the scent!"

The three dogs buried their long, wet snouts in the fabric. *Sniff, sniff, sniff!*

"Go find my babies!"

Now, Barney McCay was the lead dog. He threw his ears up in the air and got his sense of direction. "This way!" And off they went, baying into the night:

> Master, Master, coming on time!
> Master, Master, coming on time!

But that witch was still attacking those children!

"Come back here, you little crumb-snatchers!" *Boom!* "You little rug-rats!" *Boom!* Another lightning bolt hit Jack: *Pow!*

"Yeoww!" Jack screamed as he grabbed his bottom and leaped in the air. "Mary, get that corn out!"

Mary got her kernel of magic corn and threw it on the ground. A big ol' sycamore tree popped out of the ground and grew straight up into the air like Mama had said! *Chicka-boom! Chicka-boom! Boom-chicka-boom-chicka-boom-boom-boom!*

Jack and Mary climbed as quickly as they could to the uppermost branches and held on. But the ol' witch saw them.

"I gotcha now!" she chuckled as she landed her broom. She took her ax out of her belt—*Swish!*—and began to chop the tree down, singing to herself:

> Chop on the old block,
> Chop on the new block!
> Chop on the old block,
> Chop on the new block!

All of a sudden the tree began to give: *Crack!*

Jack said, "Uh-ooh!"

Crack! the tree went again.

Jack yelled out, "Barney McCay, Doodle de Doo, and Sue-Boy, your master's calling you!"

Barney McCay heard it. *Screeeeech!* He fixed his ears on the sound, and answered back:

> Master, Master, coming on time!
> Master, Master, coming on time!

Back at the scene, though, the ol' witch was chopping on that tree:

Chop on the old block,
Chop on the new block!
Chop on the old block,
Chop on the new block!

All of a sudden, the tree went, *Crack!*

Jack said, "Waaaa!"

Crack! the tree gave again.

"Whoaaa, Nellie!" Jack yelled out once more, "Barney McCay, Doodle de Doo, and Sue-Boy, your master's calling you!"

Barney McCay heard it! *Screeeeech!* The dogs stopped, and Barney McCay threw his big ol' ears into the air.

"This way, let's go!" he directed, and off the three dogs went:

Master, Master, coming on time!
Master, Master, coming on time!

Just before the tree fell, the dogs arrived at the scene.

"*Gr-r-r-r-r-r!*" They fanned out and crept toward the ol' witch.

"Nice doggies," she said as she backed off from the tree. "Sit! Stay!" she commanded, but they all suddenly leaped at the witch at the same time.

"Yeow! Ouch-ouch-ouch!" she yelled as the dogs started chewing on her. She turned and ran through the woods with the dogs in hot pursuit. Suddenly, she came to a bridge, and leaped off into the river, screaming, "Waaaaaaaaaaa!"

She dove into the water. *Splashoooooooowwwl!* The ol' hag hit the water and swam away to where the river bends.

And when that river bends, that's where this story *ends!*

STORY NOTES

In this tale, the protagonists think they're getting away with something. They set out deliberately to trick their mother—and end up in a lot of trouble! That's a very common theme, both in fiction and real-life. In fact, it's so common that it provides a perfect opportunity to encourage informal story-sharing.

As a way to "prime the pump," Bobby often tells this personal story from his own childhood:

THE LOST SHOE IN THE STORM

I can recall one classic night when sneaking out of the house against Mom's wishes brought the fury of nature itself in retribution and rebuke.

I was eleven or twelve years old. Night had fallen and it was time to come in the house. But the evening was still alive—the weather was electric (just how electric, I was to find out later). I had been playing with my friends, and we enjoyed playing hide-and-seek and dodgeball in the warm, breezy spring weather. Inevitably, our parents started to call us all in to wash up and eat, each of us slowly disappearing in a traditional game of deduction.

Well, I for one, on this particular night, had had enough. What a waste of a perfectly lovely evening to have to come in at sunset. On this specific evening, however, ominous news of a tremendous storm had saturated the airwaves. I was totally oblivious to that information, though, because I was a boy on a mission.

After dinner, I sort of dismissed myself to my room, and when everyone had departed for various parts of the house, I seized the moment to head for the door. It was all a matter of timing, and when the hallway was clear, I sprang for freedom!

I unlocked the door and stealthily shut it so it wouldn't click or bang. Finally I was out!

Free! HaHaaa!

I ran like a deer down the street! One miscalculation had occurred to me as I was running down the street, however. No one else had had the same idea as me. I was alone.

No matter—it was their loss, not mine. If they didn't have the cunning to get back outside like me—too bad!

Okay. Now I had to figure out what I could do or what game I could play alone . . . I had it! Go to Tandy Field and walk around the quadrangle.

Tandy Field is a football field in the area of North St. Louis called "The Ville." It is surrounded by Sumner High School, Tandy Recreational Center, and the Turner Middle School complex.

"Perfect idea," I thought. "It's only about a quarter of a mile from the house, and it's very pretty at night around the quadrangle."

So off I trotted, covering the quarter mile to Tandy Field. A feeling of exhilaration ran through my veins as I relished the freedom of being out after curfew and "tricking" Mom.

When I arrived at "ground zero"—the epicenter of future events—I walked alongside the limestone wall that surrounds the quad. I suddenly began to notice that the weather was beginning to change. The winds had picked up, and glancing into the sky, I marveled at the strange cloud patterns forming overhead.

Suddenly, the temperature dropped dramatically, and then all hell broke loose. The sky opened up with a deluge of rain—a sudden downpour that caught me completely off guard.

I hid under a playground gym set for several moments, contemplating my next move. The lightning flashed, producing an awesome streak of electrical current across the sky, lighting up the ominous storm clouds overhead. Then a thunderous clap resounded in the skies.

"Time to go," I reasoned immediately!

Without another moment's hesitation, I dashed from the playground and sprinted across the football field.

Big Mistake.

As I got to the 50-yard line, I realized that the field had turned to pure mud—thick, gooey, and very sticky. Now I was in the middle of the football field, ankle-deep in Missouri mud.

Ohhhh, but that was only the pitiful beginning. Lightning flashed again, and in the ensuing clap of thunder, all the lights in the area went out. Suddenly, I was in total darkness and had lost all sense of direction, what with the rain pouring in my face and eyes and all.

Panic set in, and I started hyperventilating from trying to run in a void through ankle-deep mud.

Then, it happened: as I was pulling my feet up and down in a sprint toward oblivion, my right tennis shoe came off in the mud. Here I was, standing like a crane, wondering how was I going to find this sneaker in blackness, with rain coming down in torrents.

I dropped to the ground, catching myself with both hands as I came down in the mud up to my forearms. I had gambled that if I did that, I would feel my shoe. It didn't work.

Then I groped for that accursed sneaker, in the mud and blackness and all. Try as I may, my shoe was not making itself known. A real cosmic joke, I reasoned much later. Then it happened again: lightning flashed brighter than the sun itself, night turned to day, and a nearly simultaneous clap of thunder resounded in my ears. I froze. The heavens were lit up and all the buildings around me shown in an eerie light. In that timeless moment, I looked down and saw my sneaker, the heel sticking up from the mud like a half-sunken ship.

"Aha!" I thought, and dove for my shoe, landing in a nice bed of mud on my belly and chest. I snatched that shoe from the earth just as the blackness returned.

As you can imagine, that shoe was not fit to be worn at that moment, but no matter. I scooped the mud out of it, stuffed it on my foot, and slowly plodded through the field, trying to keep both feet in my shoes this time.

Remembering what direction I was to go when night had turned to day, I instinctively headed there. After an eternity, I reached the limestone wall, the sidewalk, and the street. I ran full-out toward home, the rain washing mud from my clothes and arms as I went. I remember regretting my decision to sneak out with every stride towards home.

Arriving back at the house, I opened the front door very slowly, trying not to make it click or bang. Once inside—and out of the elements—in the quiet, warm, and *dry* sanctuary of home, I sloshed into the bathroom and wrung my clothes out. I dried off and put on a towel as if I had just gotten out of the bath, and went to my room. Flopping on the bed, I gave a big sigh of relief that it was over, and felt secure in the knowledge that it's not nice to fool Mother Nature . . . or Mother.

After these two stories, we ask the kids if *they* ever tried to get away with something, either at home or at school. There is always a general nodding of heads and a chorus of chuckles and affirmative answers— and often, a few kids will begin to tell their tales spontaneously to neighbors. That's the time to ask for one of them to tell the whole class about the experience. This isn't a formal storytelling process, simply a relating of a personal anecdote.

Kids tell some pretty incredible stories (and we hope that some of them aren't true). From innocent tales like Bobby's to much more serious accounts of theft, cheating, even violence, the kids all have experiences to relate. Many provoke laughter; others evoke horror. Sometimes it becomes obvious that a student is very proud of wrong behavior, and sees no problem with what he or she has done. At other times, we've had some poignant "confessions" as kids who are plainly repentant for their acts tell their tales. But, for the most part, we get the middle-of-the-road, comfortable, and funny stories.

We permit as many students as possible to share their stories, refraining ourselves from comments, questions, and discussion, but allowing the kids to quiz each other and talk over the consequences of their actions. We have found that, if *adults* lead these sessions, the tellers sometimes become defensive and withdrawn. But the comments and queries of the group, if they are allowed to proceed without judgmental adult interference, will often bring out significant points. Kids aren't usually reticent about asking "why": "Why did you do that? Why didn't you tell your mom? Why didn't she whip you for that, man? Why are you acting like that was all right? You know that's against the law." They're not reticent about giving opinions and passing out judgments, either—and negative judgments from peer groups can provide a stronger, more powerful stimulus for behavior change than anything a storyteller or teacher offers.

So we let the discussion take its natural direction. Of course, we do help it along when the debate gets too heated or the comments become too derogatory. And we help the students find positive ways to say what they want to say. We also make sure that key questions get answered, such as: Did you get away with it or did you get caught? If you were caught, was it by the person you were trying to trick, or by some other person or circumstance? Did you learn anything from this experience? Did you or anyone else suffer physically or emotionally from what you did?

As these questions are answered—sometimes within the story itself, sometimes in response to a question posed by a student or by one of us—we begin to see a pattern emerging. Most attempts to get away with something were not successful. Kids got caught by parents, by teachers, by their siblings. They got caught by circumstance, like Bobby's rainstorm, or a locked door, or a dropped shoe. And more often than not, the ones who suffered the most from these experiences were the storytellers themselves—from fear, from guilt, from whatever punishment parents or teachers meted out.

In other words, no one "got away with" anything. They still had their own consciences and their own values to answer to. And even the ones who swear that they got away with it now have to wonder: If "what goes around, comes around," when will it come around to me?

SOURCE NOTES

Motif B542.1.2G *Lad defeats witch with aid of dogs.* Published versions include:

"Ojo," in Fuja Abayomi, *Fourteen Hundred Cowry Shells and Other African Tales* (Lothrop & Shepard, 1971).

Janie Hunter, "Barney McKay," in Linda Goss and Marian E. Barnes, eds., *Talk that Talk: an Anthology of African-American Storytelling* (Simon & Schuster, 1989). Gullah tale.

"Wham! Slam! Jenny-Mo-Jam!" in Richard Young and Judy Dockrey Young, *Favorite Scary Stories of American Children: 23 Tales Newly Collected from Children aged 5 to 10* (August House, 1991). Variant collected by Texas folklorist Peggy Shamburger Hendricks.

Callaloo

Most of the stories in this book are intended to be told to young people; however, as this tale from Trinidad reveals, we're never too old, too rich, or too educated to be reminded of the need for love, unity, and humanity in our lives.

This is the story of a little piece of Earth. Through it flows a river. On the banks of the river live the River People. The beloved leader of the River People is called Washerwoman. She is the keeper of the clear waters of the river, a person of purity, simplicity, innocence, and generosity of spirit, as untainted of heart as the unpolluted waters of her river.

Washerwoman's example of goodness encompasses the piece of Earth completely because of a magical calabash (a container made from a dried gourd) of great power that magnifies by more than one hundred times the essence of whosoever should drink from it or bathe in its water. So Washerwoman's goodness is multiplied all over the little piece of Earth by more than one hundred times.

One day, Washerwoman is bathing by the riverside with her calabash. Her radiance fills the whole forest, reaching as far as the high woods where Papa Bois lives. Papa Bois is the father of the forest, a great and mighty spirit who never speaks a word, but who knows and understands everything. Yet even Papa Bois has never known anything as beautiful as Washerwoman bathing there by the riverside.

He takes the form of the river water, and he flows all the way down from the high woods to where she is, so as to be closer to her. When she next pours the water from the calabash over her body, Washerwoman is embraced by the spirit of Papa Bois.

She conceives a child, a boy.

Their child is born without color, as clear and translucent as the water that fathered him, as bright and dark as the reflections of the moon. He is like a mirror. The River People gaze upon this mirror in silent wonder. Some of them are dark, some are fair. There are many colors among them, black and white and brown and yellow and all sorts of other shades and mixtures as well. But each person sees simply his own self there in the child, his own reflection, his own color reflected right there in the one child. A truly wonderful understanding spreads among the River People: we are all one.

From this sense of oneness, the child receives his name. The name comes from a favorite treat among the River People, a meal of many ingredients including crabmeat all swizzled together smoothly to produce a nourishing and harmonious whole, called Callaloo.

They call the child Callaloo.

So the birth of Callaloo is a birth of understanding. The River People spend many happy years of togetherness, and they prosper. But the news of their well-being eventually reaches the ever-alert antennae of the mighty Mancrab.

Mancrab is the embodiment of man's greed and lust for power, now given form by technology. He is the corruption of man's genius, expressed in the machinery of death. Mancrab's appetite for power can never be satisfied. When word reaches him of Washerwoman and her loyal River People, he is jealous. He has always coveted the golden calabash that magnifies things one hundred times. And he covets the river for his factories.

So he challenges Washerwoman. But when he confronts Washerwoman, he encounters a power alien to him: the power of the love and trust of the River People. Fortified with this strength, Washerwoman is able to chase Mancrab away.

Furious and vengeful, Mancrab devises a clever plan. He settles secretly by the riverbank and, using his finest chemicals and oils, floods the river with a rainbow of extraordinary color. He stirs the water with promises of profit and luxury for all.

The River People are truly amazed. They run to see, and with buckets and basins they attempt to catch and keep Mancrab's illusory colors, each fighting the other for more. In their haste and greed, they leave Washerwoman unprotected, no longer surrounded by the force of their love.

Mancrab confronts her once more, and is victorious. But the victory is incomplete, for though Washerwoman lies in defeat, her goodness rises fiercely. Her unconquered spirit becomes a Bird of Fire from Paradise, flaming brighter than the sun itself.

Now you must know that neither fire nor water would harm Callaloo, for his mother is of fire and his father is of water. Only sadness of heart can kill Callaloo.

But when he hears the news of his mother's defeat, when he sees her river polluted by Mancrab's colors, and the River People quarreling and fighting, a great sadness of heart falls upon Callaloo. He is ready to leave life, to leave the little piece of Earth where man could do such wrong to man.

But before he leaves life, he has to find an explanation for man's inhumanity, which is beyond his understanding. So, weakened by sadness, each small step a great labor, Callaloo sets out to find his father who knows and understands everything.

The climb is long and hard. Callaloo stumbles and falls, but he persists, his determination conquering his weakness: he has to find an answer.

Now you remember that Papa Bois never speaks a word. When Callaloo finally reaches the high woods and calls his father's name, the answer is silence.

"Papa Bois!" he pleads. Silence is the reply. Silence all around. The forest whispers.

Only then, in complete despair, does Callaloo lie himself down on the ground to die.

At that very moment, a fretful little morocoy turtle comes up to him, scolding Callaloo for lying down in such a low and pitiful way.

"You cannot die without dignity, Callaloo. You must go to the top of the mountain and light a big fire there for all the land to see. If you must die, then walk into that fire and die like a man."

So Callaloo picks himself up with his last bit of strength and struggles to the top of the mountain. Little does he know that just as Papa Bois can flow big and wide as a river, so too can he make himself as small as a morocoy turtle.

Callaloo builds a huge fire. It burns like a cathedral on the mountaintop for all the land to see. And Callaloo walks straight into the fire, to die like a man.

The fire wraps right around him in an instant. It holds him firmly, yet the fire does not harm him. The flames that encircle Callaloo are the enfolding wings of the Bird of Fire from Paradise, the warm embrace of a mother for her son, to heal his pain and protect him.

Fire and water cannot harm him—only sadness of heart can kill Callaloo.

Callaloo's sadness leaves him. His understanding grows and his strength returns, more powerful than before. He comes down from the high woods and goes among the River People, who are still quarreling and fighting. Callaloo quiets them and begins to speak.

"We cannot go on with this arguing—it is destroying us. Instead, we must seek to understand one another. We need to respect and love this little piece of Earth we call home, and we need to respect and love each other. Our differences are there to add delight, not to divide and destroy!"

The River People look at each other in dawning understanding. They reach out to embrace each other as they listen to Callaloo.

"The true spirit of the human soul is like a circle when revealed, a circle around each human's head and heart, a circle joining every human on this little piece of Earth to every other person. The circle is a symbol of understanding, of connection and unending unity."

The River People are inspired by Callaloo. Bit by bit, they begin to delight in their differences, and to live in peace and harmony once more.

Meanwhile, Mancrab is stewing. Despite his triumph over Washerwoman, he sees the people's fascination with his colors fade; and with the fascination, so fade their quarrels and fears. Although he possesses the magical golden calabash, he soon realizes it is no match for the simple, quiet power of Callaloo and his message of love.

Mancrab is consumed by envy and hate. He plots to meet and destroy Callaloo, and he issues a challenge to battle.

On the day of combat, Mancrab lies in wait for his prey, bristling with weapons and machinery.

Callaloo comes alone and unarmed.

Mancrab gathers all his terrible and destructive power to hurl at Callaloo. He takes steady aim. But just as any man looking at Callaloo sees himself reflected there, so Mancrab sees Mancrab when he looks at Callaloo.

All his own evil and ugliness, all his own terror and destruction come rebounding back at him, magnified more than a hundred times by the golden calabash. He has nowhere to run or hide. In desperation to escape his own destruction, Mancrab spins and turns in a fury, digging himself deep into a hole in the ground.

Callaloo leaves him there and walks quietly back into the forest.

The hole in the ground can hardly contain the fury which it houses. Mancrab erupts in fits of desperation. Mancrab simply cannot understand Callaloo. And just as Callaloo that long time ago in the woods called out to Papa Bois for understanding, so does Mancrab from the depths of that hole cry out in despair to his own ancestors: *Lust, Avarice, Gluttony, Envy, Pride, Anger,* and *Sloth.*

They hear him, and the Seven Deadly Sins come to his assistance.

They come silently, invisibly, as a chorus of hoarse whispers. They whisper understanding into Mancrab's ear. "Water will not wet him. Fire will not burn him. Only sadness of heart can kill Callaloo." They explain that since Callaloo's strength is deeply rooted in his love of man, the only way to sadden Callaloo's heart is to lay waste the heart of man.

"Poison the soil," they murmur, "and the tree will surely fall. Corrupt man from within," they mutter, "and we shall be your allies. Man will fall into oblivion, and Callaloo will fall with man. Sadness of heart will kill him."

Such is the understanding provided by the Seven Deadly Sins as they whisper in Mancrab's ear. And so it happens exactly as they predict. The River People lust after the Seven Deadly Sins, forgetting all the teachings of Callaloo.

They plunder the little piece of Earth in their quest for power. They drug themselves against the fearful truth that threatens them. Their despair wears a grinning mask of indulgence as they feast and dance wildly in fancy dress to forget their worries. It is a celebration of madness. Mancrab is crowned king.

Callaloo's heart saddens; his strength begins to fade. His translucence grows dim. Callaloo's clear reflection can fade just as Mancrab's colors can fade, the strength of good and evil depending on the disposition of people.

Callaloo remembers that time long ago on the mountaintop, and resolves not to fall. But man can be cruel. And the people, lost to power, become heartlessly cruel. They go out in search of Callaloo and find him, sad and weakened. They do not see their reflections in him; his strength is gone.

The people take Callaloo and set him down as a spectacle, then offer him up to King Mancrab!

Mancrab feasts his eyes greedily upon the defeated Callaloo, and demands that Callaloo must bow before him. But still Callaloo stands.

Mancrab assembles his mighty rage and force, then rises high and higher, towering above the throng to fell Callaloo to the ground.

Then in an instant, there is a blinding flash of light, brighter than the sun itself. A Bird of Fire from Paradise sets down a circle of protection around her beloved son. In the next instant after the flash, the people behold a band of little children holding hands right around Callaloo.

The sight of this circle of innocence touches the small spark of humanity left in them. They turn as one and drive Mancrab away.

And so it is on the little piece of Earth. The people remain torn between corruption and understanding. Mancrab plots while Callaloo stands with a circle of children his only hope and protection.

And so it will be until the people remember that **we are all one**. Papa Bois whispers in our ear. The Bird of Fire takes wing in our hearts. And though sadness of heart can kill Callaloo, and the little piece of earth yet languishes in fear and despair, we still cling to that one spark of hope. It is brighter than the sun itself.

So our story ends. So our story begins.

STORY NOTES

The profound metaphors in this story encompass not only the spiritual world, but also the technological, environmental, political, and historical spheres. Personal responsibility and moral/ethical issues facing people today are interwoven throughout the tale of a boy born of a woman pure in spirit and a father who moves through the wind, water, earth, and sun. The story has echoes of George Lucas's *Star Wars*, invoking the eternal struggle between good and evil on a metaphorical and scientific level.

The audience age range for "Callaloo" is fourteen through adult. It works well with teens who love to read and have the creativity to react to stories whether on the screen, in books, or in performances—with active imaginations.

The tale should be read slowly, allowing time to assimilate and internalize the concepts. It will do no good to try "Evelyn Woods reading dynamics" on this piece. Every time a new character appears, that figure needs to be pondered and visualized. Stopping to reflect on the story's characters gives the reader time to equate the knowledge, skills, and abilities of each character to a personal frame of reference.

We find that readers' theater is an effective way to share the story with a class (a script follows, on page 117). In this manner, the tale seems to unfold with clarity and force. After reading the story aloud to the class, and before moving on to readers' theater, a question-and-answer session would help explore and clarify images and metaphors. The Seven Deadly Sins should be analyzed closely, and students asked to discuss how they view each so-called "sin" and how it affects the peace and harmony of their neighborhood, their school, city, state, country, and ultimately, the planet. Is pollution of the earth, water, and air an issue that should be focused on? Should students be concerned about the depletion of the ozone layer, causing harmful ultra-violet radiation to melt polar caps and causing floods and droughts? How do the "illusory" colors tempt and trick the River People to become selfish and greedy?

THE PLAYERS

Callaloo is a Christ figure, or might be equated to Adam, Eve, and the progeny that succeeded human beings from the earliest existence in East Africa to all the continents of the earth.

Papa Bois is considered the male part of the existence, represented by omniscience and a complete consciousness of the universe. In this story that seems to continue into perpetuity, Papa Bois at some point had a *first* meeting with Washerwoman and started the cycle that runs throughout human evolution on a physical and spiritual level.

Washerwoman could be the Blessed Virgin Mary in archetype, or the feminine *cause* in Nature that nurtures, grows, and lives a vibrant, loving existence.

The River People represent all the races on Earth.

Mancrab personifies some unscrupulous, multinational corporations, compromising and polluting the environment with industrial waste.

The Seven Deadly Sins represent the pollution of the human spirit, which is compromised by weaknesses of the flesh and pursuits of pleasure, devolving into excesses and excursions into the dark side of the psyche and feeding the shadow:

Anger: arguments, fights, ill will, waste of life force projecting hateful energy to another

Lust: sexual perversion, waste of focus through uncontrolled desires

Avarice: stealing, robbing, killing, dishonesty, deceit

Gluttony: overindulgence of appetites, lack of self control

Envy: ill will, revenge, waste of life-force hating or disliking someone

Pride: refusal to admit fault, superiority complex

Sloth: laziness, slovenly habits, uninspired and apathetic behavior

SOURCE NOTES

This story is related to Motifs A1388.1 *Hatred released among mankind;* A1614 *Origin of races;* Z71.5.6.2 *The Seven Deadly Sins;* and Z110 *Personification (of good, evil, etc.)*

Bobby adapted this folktale from a story in Caribbean dialect collected by Peter Minshall of Trinidad. He first performed it in 1988 at the St. Louis Art Museum in connection with the *Caribbean Festival Arts* exhibit after being introduced to the original work by the late Richard Gaugert.

Callaloo stew is described in the story when the child is born. It is a staple of the Caribbean people, used for nourishment as we eat beef stew in America. Metaphorically, the stew represents the assimilation of the peoples of the Earth into one whole, *Homo Sapiens,* and recalls the image of America as a "melting pot" of immigrants.

Callaloo:
Readers' Theater Script

THE PLAYERS

Narrator
River People
Washerwoman
Papa Bois
Callaloo
Mancrab
Seven Deadly Sins

Narrator:

This is the story of a little piece of Earth. Through it flows a river. On the banks of the river live the River People. The beloved leader of the River People is called Washerwoman. She is the keeper of the clear waters of the river, a person of purity, simplicity, innocence, and generosity of spirit, as untainted of heart as the unpolluted waters of her river.

Washerwoman:

I am Washerwoman. My example of goodness encompasses the piece of Earth completely because of a magical calabash of great power that magnifies by more than one hundred times the essence of whoso-ever should drink from it or bathe in its water. My goodness is multi-plied all over the little piece of Earth by more than one hundred times.

One day, I am bathing by the riverside with my calabash. My radi-ance fills the whole forest, reaching as far as the high woods where Papa Bois lives.

Papa Bois:

I am Papa Bois, the father of the forest, a great and mighty spirit who never speaks a word, but who knows and understands everything. Yet even I have never known anything as beautiful as Washerwoman bathing there by the riverside.

I take the form of the river water, and flow all the way down from the high woods to where she is, so as to be closer to her.

When she next pours the water from the calabash over her body, Washerwoman is embraced by my spirit: the spirit of Papa Bois.

Washerwoman:

I conceive a child, a boy.

Narrator:

Their child is born without color, as clear and translucent as the water that fathered him, as bright and dark as the reflections of the moon. He is like a mirror.

River People:

We, the River People, gaze upon this mirror in silent wonder. Some of us are dark, some are fair. There are many colors among us, black and white and brown and yellow and all sorts of other shades and mix-tures as well. But each of us sees simply our own self there in the child, our own reflection, our own color reflected right there in the one child. A truly wonderful understanding spreads among us: **we are all one.**

From this sense of oneness, we name the child. The name comes from a favorite treat among us, a meal of many ingredients including crabmeat all swizzled together smoothly to produce a nourishing and harmonious whole, called Callaloo.

We call the child Callaloo.

Narrator:

So the birth of Callaloo is a birth of understanding. The River People spend many happy years of togetherness, and they prosper. But the news of their well-being eventually reaches the ever-alert antennae of the mighty Mancrab.

Mancrab:

I am the embodiment of man's greed and lust for power, now given form by technology. I am the corruption of man's genius, expressed in the machinery of death. My appetite for power can never be satisfied. When word reaches me of Washerwoman and her loyal River People, I am jealous. I have always coveted the golden calabash that magnifies things one hundred times. And I covet the river for my factories.

So I challenge Washerwoman.

Narrator:

But when he confronts Washerwoman, he encounters a power alien to him: the power of the love and trust of the River People. Fortified with this strength, Washerwoman is able to chase Mancrab away.

Furious and vengeful, Mancrab devises a clever plan.

Mancrab:

I settle secretly by the riverbank and, using my finest chemicals and oils, flood the river with a rainbow of extraordinary color. I stir the water with promises of profit and luxury for all.

River People:

We are truly amazed! We run to see, and with buckets and basins we attempt to catch and keep Mancrab's illusory colors, each fighting the other for more. In our haste and greed, we leave Washerwoman unprotected, no longer surrounded by the force of our love.

Narrator:

Mancrab confronts Washerwoman once more, and is victorious. But the victory is incomplete, for though Washerwoman lies in defeat, her goodness rises fiercely. Her unconquered spirit becomes a Bird of Fire from Paradise, flaming brighter than the sun itself.

Now you must know that neither fire nor water would harm Callaloo, for his mother is of fire and his father is of water. Only sadness of heart can kill Callaloo.

Callaloo:

Yes, only sadness of heart can kill me. But when I hear the news of my mother's defeat, when I see her river polluted by Mancrab's colors, and the River People quarreling and fighting, a great sadness of heart falls upon me. I am ready to leave life, to leave the little piece of Earth where man could do such wrong to man.

But before I leave life, I have to find an explanation for man's inhumanity, which is beyond my understanding. So, weakened by sadness, each small step a great labor, I set out to find my father who knows and understands everything.

The climb is long and hard. I stumble and fall, but I persist, my determination conquering my weakness: I have to find an answer.

Narrator:

Now you remember that Papa Bois never speaks a word. When Callaloo finally reaches the high woods and calls his father's name, the answer is silence.

Callaloo

Papa Bois!

Narrator:

Silence is the reply. Silence all around. The forest whispers.

124

Callaloo:

Only then, in complete despair, do I lie myself down on the ground to die.

Narrator:

At that very moment, a fretful little morocoy turtle comes up to him, scolding Callaloo for lying down in such a low and pitiful way, without dignity. He tells him that he must go to the top of the mountain and light a big fire there for all the land to see. Then, says the turtle, if Callaloo must die, he must walk into that fire and die like a man.

Callaloo:

So I pick myself up with my last bit of strength and struggle to the top of the mountain.

Papa Bois:

Little does Callaloo know that just as Papa Bois can flow big and wide as a river, so too can he make himself as small as a morocoy turtle.

Callaloo:

I build a huge fire. It burns like a cathedral on the mountaintop for all the land to see. And I walk straight into the fire, to die like a man.

The fire wraps right around me in an instant. It holds me firmly, yet the fire does not harm me!

Washerwoman:

The flames that encircle Callaloo are the enfolding wings of the Bird of Fire from Paradise, the warm embrace of a mother for her son, to heal his pain and protect him.

Narrator:

Fire and water cannot harm him—only sadness of heart can kill Callaloo.

Callaloo:

My sadness leaves me. My understanding grows and my strength returns, more powerful than before. I come down from the high woods and go among the River People, who are still quarreling and fighting. I quiet them and begin to speak.

"We cannot go on with this arguing—it is destroying us. Instead, we must seek to understand one another. We need to respect and love this little piece of Earth we call home, and we need to respect and love each other. Our differences are there to add delight, not to divide and destroy!"

River People:

We look at each other in dawning understanding. We reach out to embrace each other as we listen to Callaloo.

Callaloo:

"The true spirit of the human soul is like a circle when revealed, a circle around each human's head and heart, a circle joining every human on this little piece of Earth to every other person. The circle is a symbol of understanding, of connection and unending unity."

River People:

We are inspired by Callaloo. Bit by bit, we begin to delight in our differences, and to live in peace and harmony once more.

Mancrab:

Meanwhile, I am stewing. Despite my triumph over Washerwoman, I see the people's fascination with my colors fade; and with the fascination, so fade their quarrels and fears. Although I possess the magical golden calabash, I soon realize it is no match for the simple, quiet power of Callaloo and his message of love.

I am consumed by envy and hate. I plot to meet and destroy Callaloo, and I issue a challenge to battle.

Narrator:

On the day of combat, Mancrab lies in wait for his prey, bristling with weapons and machinery. Callaloo comes alone and unarmed.

Mancrab:

I gather all my terrible and destructive power to hurl at Callaloo. I take steady aim.

Narrator:

But just as any man looking at Callaloo sees himself reflected there, so Mancrab sees Mancrab when he looks at Callaloo. All his own evil and ugliness, all his own terror and destruction come rebounding back at him, magnified more than a hundred times by the golden calabash.

Mancrab:

I have nowhere to run or hide. In desperation to escape my own destruction, I spin and turn in a fury, digging myself deep into a hole in the ground.

Callaloo:

I leave him there and walk quietly back into the forest.

Narrator:

The hole in the ground can hardly contain the fury which it houses. Mancrab erupts in fits of desperation.

Mancrab:

(Howling) I cannot understand Callaloo!

Narrator:

And just as Callaloo that long time ago in the woods called out to Papa Bois for understanding, so does Mancrab from the depths of that hole cry out in despair to his own ancestors.

Mancrab:

Lust, Avarice, Gluttony, Envy, Pride, Anger, and Sloth!

Seven Deadly Sins:

We hear him, and we come to his assistance. We come silently, invisibly, as a chorus of hoarse whispers. We whisper understanding into Mancrab's ear. "Water will not wet him. Fire will not burn him. Only sadness of heart can kill Callaloo." We explain that since Callaloo's strength is deeply rooted in his love of man, the only way to sadden Callaloo's heart is lay waste the heart of man.

"Poison the soil," we murmur, "and the tree will surely fall. Corrupt man from within," we mutter, "and we shall be your allies. Man will fall into oblivion, and Callaloo will fall with man. Sadness of heart will kill him."

Such is the understanding we provide as we whisper in Mancrab's ear. And so it happens exactly as we predict. The River People lust after us, the Seven Deadly Sins, forgetting all the teachings of Callaloo.

River People:

We plunder the little piece of Earth in our quest for power. We drug ourselves against the fearful truth that threatens us. Our despair wears a grinning mask of indulgence as we feast and dance wildly in fancy dress to forget our worries. It is a celebration of madness. Mancrab is crowned king.

Callaloo:

My heart saddens; my strength begins to fade. My translucence grows dim. My clear reflection can fade just as Mancrab's colors can fade, the strength of good and evil depending on the disposition of people.

Narrator:

Callaloo remembers that time long ago on the mountaintop, and resolves not to fall. But man can be cruel. And the people, lost to

128

power, become heartlessly cruel. They go out in search of Callaloo and find him, sad and weakened. They do not see their reflections in him; his strength is gone.

The people take Callaloo and set him down as a spectacle, then offer him up to King Mancrab!

Mancrab feasts his eyes greedily upon the defeated Callaloo. It is his finest hour!

Mancrab:

Bow before me, Callaloo!

Callaloo:

But still I stand.

Mancrab:

I assemble my mighty rage and force, then rise high and higher, towering above the throng to fell Callaloo to the ground.

Washerwoman:

Then in an instant, there is a blinding flash of light, brighter than the sun itself. I appear as a Bird of Fire from Paradise and set down a circle of protection around my beloved son. In the next instant after the flash, the people behold a band of little children holding hands right around Callaloo.

River People:

The sight of this circle of innocence touches the small spark of humanity left in us. We turn as one and drive Mancrab away.

Narrator:

And so it is on the little piece of Earth. The people remain torn between corruption and understanding. Mancrab plots while Callaloo stands with a circle of children his only hope and protection.

River People:

And so it will be until the people remember that **we are all one**. Papa Bois whispers in our ear. The Bird of Fire takes wing in our hearts. And though sadness of heart can kill Callaloo, and the little piece of Earth yet languishes in fear and despair, we still cling to that one spark of hope. It is brighter than the sun itself.

All:

So our story ends. So our story begins.

3

Storytelling as an Experiential Approach to Character Education

As we have explored in this book, telling stories to children is an effective way to instill an appreciation and understanding of the behaviors that our society values. The discussions and activities that are suggested can further enhance children's comprehension and acceptance of these virtues. But listening, discussing, and understanding are not enough without action. To develop responsibility, young people need to *have* responsibility. To learn to care, they need to perform caring actions. For this reason, educators advocate the "experiential approach."

In *The Moral Intelligence of Children*, Robert Coles discusses the need for children to "live out" their values: to turn nouns such as patience, courtesy, respect, and compassion into verbs, words of action. He urges us—storytellers, educators, parents—to "take those nouns that denote good moral traits and turn them into verbs: tasks to accomplish, plans for action, to be followed by the actual work of doing."[1]

Storytelling can provide that experiential approach. Coles asserts that imagined scenarios, like those within a tale, set the stage for later actions by allowing the child to experience the scenario and its consequences through the imagination. Further, in the act of listening to stories being told, children actually practice the virtues of courtesy and attentiveness. They are considerate of other listeners and respectful of the storyteller, and they are encouraged to show appreciation for the story and the teller with politeness.

These experiences can be further enhanced by teaching the children themselves to tell stories:

In the process of learning to tell, students learn to listen attentively not only to the teller, but to each other. They learn to be respectful of each other, building each other's confidence and trust by responding in positive, helpful ways. They learn to show appreciation and acceptance of other students' creativity.

In the process of finding their stories, students learn about the traditions and values of other cultures, and learn to recognize, appreciate and respect the differences and similarities of all people.

In the process of preparing their stories, students learn to explore their own creativity, and to trust their ability to bring a tale to life for others.

Students also learn to help and support each other as they work cooperatively towards crafting successful storytelling performances.

In the process of telling their stories, students learn the joy of giving pleasure to others through their own hard work. They also learn to respect their audience by choosing appropriate tales and sharing them in appropriate ways.

We have seen all of these results again and again in the **Kaleidoscope** storytelling residencies that we teach in classrooms across the country. Whether kindergarten or junior high students, the youngsters learn to listen attentively to each other, to treat each other with respect, and ultimately to trust each other. They help classmates work towards common goals. They are understanding and sensitive to others' weaknesses, patient with mistakes, and eager to point out and celebrate successes. They learn to care.

We believe that these same results can be achieved in *any* class-room—but it's not as easy as simply following a lesson plan. In fact, as with all successful character education, the key to success is not the facts you teach or the lesson plan you follow, but the attitude you display and the behaviors you model.

Here's what we do.

Kaleidoscope is hands-on and highly interactive, with students learning by *doing* and *experiencing success*. There are only two rules in this class, but we emphasize and enforce them:

Students must *listen* to the instructors *and* to each other.

Students must be *supportive* of each other.

These rules are reiterated throughout the class, and the result is an atmosphere of peer affirmation and trust: a safe environment for creativity.

It's important that students understand that they *can* be storytellers—and that each of them will and *should* do it differently. So we start by asking who in the class is a storyteller already. The younger they are, the more hands go up; kindergartners know instinctively that they are storytellers, while teens think more in terms of "performance" and keep their hands down. We help all of them understand that all of us are natural storytellers, that we all tell stories all of the time as we communicate with others. We also point out that, just as we all have different styles of communication, we all have different styles of storytelling, and that each person's style is right for him or her. This is an important thing to teach—that diversity is not only okay, but essential. (It applies in life, too.)

As long as we're talking about differences, we go on to discuss the way in which listeners create different images as they listen to the same story. Not only is the image in each person's mind unique, but it also is "perfect"—the right image for that listener to create. Understanding this concept allows the students to explore and express their creativity as they become storytellers.

We explain that a storyteller is "the director of the Theater of the Mind." Now, film directors make decisions about who will be cast, where the action will take place, and other details of character motivation and the script itself. The same applies to the director of the Theater of the Mind. The storyteller gets to make decisions about characters, setting, and motivation in the stories that he or she tells.

Now it's time to tell a story. We instruct the students to put down anything they may have in their hands or lap, and simply to listen to the tale and be aware of the images that they are creating in their minds. The story we often use is a skeletal version of "The Little Girl and the Gunniwolf," a simple African-American folktale found in many collections[2]:

> Once upon a time there was a little girl who lived way out at the edge of the jungle. Now every day, that little girl's momma said to her, "Little Girl, don't you go near the jungle, 'cause if you do, the Gunniwolf's gonna get you!"
>
> And every day, that little girl said, "Yes, Momma, I know. I won't go near the jungle."
>
> And she never did.
>
> One day, that little girl's momma said, "Little Girl, I have to go into the village to get some groceries. Now, while I'm

134

gone, you may play inside the house, or behind the house, or in front of the house. But remember: don't you go near the jungle, 'cause if you do, the Gunniwolf's gonna get you!"

And that little girl said, "Yes, Momma, I know. I won't go near the jungle!"

So her momma went off to the village.

While she was gone, the little girl played inside the house, and behind the house, and in front of the house. While she was skipping in circles around the house, she saw some beautiful white flowers, growing *right at the edge* of the jungle.

"Oooh!" she said. "Those white flowers would make a beautiful bouquet for my momma!" So she went over and she picked 'em. And as she picked, she sang a little song:

> Kum-ki, kum-kwa
> Kum-ki, kum-kwa
> Kum-ki, kum-kwa

Then, she saw some lovely pink flowers, growing *just inside* the jungle.

"Oooh!" she said. "Those pink flowers would make a lovely bouquet for my momma!" So she went in and she picked them.

> Kum-ki, kum-kwa
> Kum-ki, kum-kwa
> Kum-ki, kum-kwa

Then, she saw some gorgeous red flowers, growing *right in the middle* of the jungle.

"Oooh! Those red flowers would make a gorgeous bouquet for my momma!" So she went in and she picked them.

> Kum-ki, kum-kwa
> Kum-ki, kum-kwa
> Kum-ki, kum-kwa

Just then, right in front of her, she saw the Gunniwolf!

"Little girl! Why do you move?"

"I no move!"

"Then sing your little song again!"

So the little girl sang:

Kum-ki, kum-kwa

Kum-ki, kum-kwa

Kum-ki, kum-kwa

And the Gunniwolf went fast asleep!

So the little girl went tippy-toe, tippy-toe, tippy-toe away from the Gunniwolf. But the Gunniwolf woke up!

Hunkacha! Hunkacha! Hunkacha!

"Little girl! Why do you move?"

"I no move!"

"Then sing your little song again!"

So the little girl sang:

Kum-ki, kum-kwa

Kum-ki, kum-kwa

Kum-ki, kum-kwa

But the Gunniwolf did not go to sleep, so she tried again:

Kum-ki, kum-kwa

Kum-ki, kum-kwa

Kum-ki, kum-kwa

And the Gunniwolf went fast asleep.

So the little girl went tippy-toe, tippy-toe, tippy-toe . . . tippy-toe, tippy-toe, tippy-toe away from the Gunniwolf.

But the Gunniwolf woke up!

Hunkacha! Hunkacha! Hunkacha!

"Little girl! Why do you move?"

"I no move!"

"Then sing your little song again!"

So the little girl sang:

Kum-ki, kum-kwa
Kum-ki, kum-kwa
Kum-ki, kum-kwa

But the Gunniwolf did not go to sleep, so she tried again:

Kum-ki, kum-kwa
Kum-ki, kum-kwa
Kum-ki, kum-kwa

He *still* didn't go to sleep, so she tried one more time:

Kum-ki, kum-kwa
Kum-ki, kum-kwa
Kum-ki, kum-kwa

And the Gunniwolf *finally* went fast asleep.
So the little girl ran tippy-toe, tippy-toe, tippy-toe . . .
tippy-toe, tippy-toe, tippy-toe . . .
tippy-toe, tippy-toe, tippy-toe . . .
And the Gunniwolf never did wake up!
So if you ever go near that jungle, remember to sing that
little song, and the Gunniwolf will never, ever, *ever* get you!
And that's that.

Following the story, listeners are engaged in a visualization exercise designed to help them develop concrete images of the characters and setting of the tale. Students close their eyes as we take them back and ask questions to help them "see" the story clearly. "First look at the child in the tale. How old is she? How tall is she? How much does she weigh? What color is her skin? What color are her eyes? What is she wearing?" We do the same for each character in the story, then for the setting. We ask students to visualize the house, the clearing in front of the house, and the jungle. As we talk, we also encourage them to branch out: "Now, in the story, the danger takes place in the jungle, but you might want it to be somewhere else. It could be a forest or a haunted house or the ocean . . . wherever you want it to be . . ."

They are encouraged to create images that speak to them personally, and these do not have to conform to storybook pictures or to the images described by the teller. (You may have noticed that the version of the Gunniwolf we retold here has no description at all. That's so listeners can envision their own characters freely, without conflicting information.)

During this process, the kids also are urged to explore the motivations of the characters through open-ended questions: "Why do you think the little girl went into the woods even though her mother warned her not to? In the story, she was picking flowers, but you might think that's kind of lame. Why would *you* go into known danger?"

Finally, students are encouraged to explore what the story means to them, to look through their personal "kaleidoscopes." They are assured that there is no right or wrong way to tell the story, and that their own ways will be "perfect" for them. (There is one caveat: the little girl must get home safely. Tellers can create danger, but they must find a way out. This is a good problem-solving exercise.)

After the visualization exercise, students have chances to share their new versions of the story with partners, and to get positive feedback from them and from the group. We ask the kids to pair off. In each pair, one person becomes the teller, and one the listener. The teller tells his or her story. We remind everyone that this is indeed a brand-new version, so it won't be polished yet. The teller might forget some parts, or may not have found the exact words to use yet—but the images are what's important.

The listener has an important job, too. He or she must listen actively and attentively, making eye contact and showing interest. Listeners must also note two or three things they particularly like about these new stories—descriptions of the little girl, ways tellers use their voices to portray different characters, or other features. They are reminded of the class's two rules—listen to each other and be supportive.

After the tellers have shared their tales, the group is brought back together and the listeners report to the group the two or three things

138

that they liked about the story. This is a really powerful exercise. As the listeners report, their tellers get to hear good things about their creative efforts shared with the entire group. They realize that the listener was really paying attention, too. Often, the listener recounts the story in vivid detail, which is a real affirmation for the teller. And just as often, the entire class responds with positive comments and chuckles that provide group affirmation.

It's important for the instructor to add a few comments to each report, as well. This is a "teachable moment" when you can build on experience to teach rather than lecture about theory. For example, when a listener reports enjoying the sound effects the teller used, we comment on the effectiveness of using sounds to enhance the story and bring it to life.

After all of the listeners report, we reverse the process, asking the listeners to become tellers and the tellers to listen. We report again, following the same procedure. It's always fun to hear all the different versions of the story, and to use the opportunity to emphasize that each teller and story was unique and each one was "perfect."

Now, it's true that some students will have created stories for shock value—gross, violent, or sexual in nature. The older the students, the more likely you are to encounter this. They will try to test you, and to test your rule about being supportive and saying only positive things. But in all the thousands of times we've heard versions of this story, we've never heard one that completely crossed the line. That's not to say that the version that was told to the listener didn't cross the line, but the listener has always—and we emphasize ALWAYS—edited the report so that the contents are understood but not explicit. The teller will watch us closely as the listener reports, with that little smile that says, "Let's see what you do with this!" And we have always been able to laugh (and groan) and lift our eyebrows in acknowledgment of the teller's efforts, then shake our heads and say, "Okay . . . well, that was creative! I'm glad you found a way to save the little girl from drowning in all the snot and excrement. That really must have smelled bad—how did she get the smell off so her mother didn't notice? Oh, and listener—thank you for your very careful report. I appreciate your tactfulness." The kids laugh, the creative teller realizes that he or she didn't "get us," and the class moves on.

We've actually learned to appreciate such tellers, because they help us prove to everyone how everyone's version is "perfect" for him or her. Some tellers have a need to push and test our acceptance, and they find creative ways to do it within the parameters of the class. Their tales really *are* perfect! By the way, we have realized over the years that the kids who test us are often the ones who have had very negative and unsuccessful experiences in school. When they develop what they expect to be an inappropriate story, it seems to be an excuse for failing yet again: "I knew I couldn't do it—now, I can quit." But by accepting their story, we give them successful experiences, and they are taken by surprise. They also lose their excuse for quitting, and we often watch these kids become our best allies and storytellers.

In this exercise, students have learned to trust their own creative visions and to accept and celebrate the creative offerings of others. By fashioning their own characters, settings, and motivations for the story, the students have become part of the oral tradition, molding the tale to meet their own needs.

They have officially become storytellers.

A note here about the role of creativity in character education: creativity is a process that enables divergent thinking, openmindedness to new ideas, and increased understanding and change. These are the skills that help children to become more effective problem-solvers by developing and evaluating a variety of solutions; to appreciate and tolerate different perspectives; and to gain self-esteem. Clearly, creativity is a "power tool" for character education!

Another part of the process is helping students identify appropriate stories to tell, then bringing tales to life through group, small-group, and individual exercises which develop voices, gestures, body language, and facial expression. During all of the exercises, the same two rules are enforced: listening, supporting. Students are encouraged to clap for the efforts of their peers and to pay attention to each other. They are not allowed to put each other down or to make fun of each other. It takes patience on the part of the instructor, and a constant reiteration and interpretation of the rules to make this happen. It requires that the leader provide the model, offering positive comments and encouragement rather than criticisms. It is the only way we know to create a safe environment for learning.

As the students prepare their stories, they will receive coaching from the instructor and from the group. Again, we emphasize that comments must be positive—at this stage, it doesn't help to be told what's wrong. As students break into small groups to listen to and coach each other, the instructors circulate and coach the listeners ("Look at your teller") and the tellers ("You haven't forgotten, you're just distracted. Now, concentrate. What was Mr. Fox doing when Lady Mary saw him?"). The instructors' behavior must model and embody the rules for the students.

The performance is an essential element of the project, giving students a goal to work towards and an achievement to celebrate. It's also scary! As instructors, we want the performance to be as trauma-free as possible, and to be a moment of success rather than failure. For that reason, we spend a lot of time helping students combat stage-fright and emphasizing the importance of that "safe space" that they must create for each other.

The hardest part of performance for many folks (young and old) happens before the performance actually begins. It's that awkward thousand-year-long moment when you walk from your seat to the center of the stage. The audience itself can help to alleviate the problem by being supportive—so we make sure that the storytelling students know how to support each other even in those pre-performance moments.

We start by showing the students exactly where they will be performing their stories. Of course, we choose a place with few distractions for both the teller and the audience, and try to create as much privacy as possible for this first experience. We show them where the "audience" will sit and where the performance space will be. Then we tell them exactly what will happen on the day of the performances:

"On Friday, you will each be telling your story to the entire group. Before we begin, we'll do some warm-up exercises, and a visualization exercise so that you can review your story. Then, I'll call the name of the first teller. We've already drawn numbers for the order of telling, so you know when you'll be telling and you know what to expect. When your name is called, come up and take your place. As you walk up, we will all clap. Take a deep breath, review in your mind the first line of the story while you make eye contact with the audience, then tell your story. When the story is over, we will all applaud. Stay up here and allow us to applaud for you—we want to show you our appreciation for your story. Then we'll ask the audience to tell you what they liked about your story. Stay up here so we can tell you to your face what we liked. We'll only be offering positive comments, so there's nothing to worry about! Then we'll clap as you sit down, and the next name will be called."

Then we practice. First, we ask about half the class to stand, facing the other half. They are instructed to keep their hands at their side, stop twitching, and make eye contact. Of course, the "audience" half of the class must make eye contact, too. The hardest part of this exercise is to stop the giggling—from both halves of the group. But we've found that if we wait patiently, the giggling will stop, and it won't happen on performance day. So we wait until everyone is under control before switching roles.

Then we acknowledge how awkward that walk to the stage can be. It's the time when you're most vulnerable, when everyone's eyes are on you, and you have nothing to offer. Just you, walking . . . maybe tripping . . . maybe knocking over a chair. It's excruciating for anyone who is the least bit self-conscious, but it is a whole lot easier if everyone claps while you do it. For some psychological reason, that clapping feels protective and distractive—and seems to lessen the walk by about nine hundred miles.

One by one, we ask the students to "take the stage." They are instructed to come to the center of the performance space while everyone claps, make eye contact, and say their own names and the titles of the stories they are going to tell. Then they wait for the applause to begin before they return to their seats.

This gets really monotonous, and your hands feel as if they are going to fall off from clapping (we usually take twenty-second breaks between every seven or eight students). The instructor has to remind the audience over and over again to clap. But this seemingly trivial exercise gets surprising results. Students feel more confident after getting past that hurdle, and when performance day comes, no one has to be reminded to clap. It comes automatically and enthusiastically, because the kids all know how important it is.

This should be only the first formal performance, not the last. It's important to provide many opportunities for student storytellers to share and perfect their new skills. Besides, they need chances to give something valuable to fellow students and to the community. They can tell stories to children in lower grades, enhancing the curriculum, motivating other kids to read, and providing entertainment. They can swap stories with classes on their own grade level, or even with upper grades when the story fits into a curriculum theme. They can tell stories at PTA meetings, retirement centers, community centers, preschools, libraries, even festivals. And each time, they will learn the joy of sharing and giving back to the community.

As these storytelling venues are arranged, it's important to discuss appropriate choices with the student tellers. For example, when fifth graders tell to the first grade, the older kids must be helped to understand which stories in their collective repertoire will be understood and appreciated by their audience. Fifth graders often think it would be cool to tell a really scary story to the youngsters. We explain to them the need to be responsible to their audience, and we help them learn to choose stories that will respect the children's needs.

Does all this really work? Yes, it really does. It works in the most unlikely circumstances, with the most unlikely kids.

In the fall of 1996, we were privileged to fill a month-long vacancy in the Spiritual Life Program at Alaska Children's Services, Inc., a psychiatric residential treatment center for severely emotionally disturbed children and adolescents. The primary focus of the Spiritual Life Program is storytelling, helping the students explore and evaluate parts of their lives that deal with values through folktales from around the world.

As we worked with these students (all of whom had extensive histories of abuse, severe emotional disturbance, and multiple experiences with the juvenile justice system), we were increasingly conscious of the need to prevent peer abuse, establish some norms of respect and kindness, and build self-esteem. Storytelling helped, discussions enhanced, but we needed to *do*.

One day, we decided to try teaching the kids to *tell* stories, rather than simply listen and discuss. Now, this program is a strictly voluntary one, in which the students can choose whether or not to participate. These are not young people who have experienced success in school, or who feel comfortable in their own skins. We had no idea how our proposal would be greeted. They could have just walked away, so we approached with extreme caution.

To our surprise and joy, the response in all seven groups was positive. They were willing to give it a try, and no one walked! We assured them that the telling was completely voluntary, and we laid out the rules: listen, be positive. They agreed. We told the story, went through the visualization exercise, and then asked if anyone would like to share his or her version of the story (there were never more than seven students per group, and pairing off was strictly forbidden, so group sharing was not only possible but mandatory).

In each group, the scenario was the same. They looked at each other warily. They looked at the floor. We reiterated that no one would be forced to tell, but that if somebody did choose to do so, we would all follow the rules: listen, be positive. Eventually, a volunteer would emerge.

These kids had wonderful imaginations, and few opportunities to use them in positive ways. Once they trusted that the rules would be enforced, they were eager to try out their stories. And they were just as eager to listen to each other and give praise. "Hey, man, that was a real cool story." "You were real brave to go first, man." "Great sound effects. Hey—can I go next?"

It was remarkable to see the looks of pride as the tellers received praise from their peers. They were both proud and humble, and willing to share the limelight, urging others to tell their own stories.

144

One of the most memorable moments occurred in the cabin housing the oldest students (ages fifteen to eighteen). During all of the sessions with this group, one young man sat curled in a fetal position on the couch as he listened. The only response we ever received from him was a periodic slight tilt of the head with one eye peering out, denoting interest and cautious approval. All of us—students and storytellers alike—were amazed when he was the first to volunteer to tell his story.

As he rose to stand in front of the group, his peers exchanged startled looks, then quickly settled to total silence to listen. His story was vivid, told with clarity and brevity. All of us clapped enthusiastically, then watched as he returned to his fetal position. When the applause ended, we heard him mumble, "Man, I just made a fool of myself. Just made a fool of myself." He curled even more tightly into himself, rocking a bit as the students stared at him in denial.

Then support came from the most unlikely source in the room. The biggest, toughest, most belligerent one of them all spoke quietly but emphatically, "No you didn't, Man. You a hero. It took guts to get up in front of us and tell that story. You a hero."

The others chimed in, echoing their leader and adding comments of praise for the story itself. Gradually, we watched him uncurl. He looked warily around, then nodded in acceptance of their words.

No one followed him. There seemed to be a general agreement that his accomplishment should be allowed to stand alone. Instead, they discussed his story a bit more, and talked about their own fears of public speaking, then asked one of us to finish the session with another story. The mood was one of solemn celebration.

It's hard to describe that scene even now without feeling the awe that it inspired that day. It cannot be emphasized enough that peer support was virtually unknown among this group. Rarely did a session begin before a fight was broken up; rarely did one end without insults being hurled. But that day, we saw a change that was to last throughout the rest of our stay.

Usually, the session following such an emotional event is anti-climactic. But not this time. Our topic that day was "heroes," and we had a discussion about heroism during which we posed several questions: What is a hero? Do you have a hero in your own life? Have you ever been a hero for someone else? The answers were poignant. They named younger brothers who helped them cope with drug and alcohol hazes; aunts and sisters who came to their aid when they were being abused by fathers, uncles, and grandparents; friends. These were kids to whom the word "hero" had real meaning.

When we asked them if they had ever been a hero for others, the room fell silent. Then, one by one, they acknowledged occasions when they had been there for others. Everyone except our friend in the fetal position: when his turn came he shook his head without lifting it from his knees. "No way. I ain't a hero. Only thing people ever wanna do with me is put me in jail. I ain't no hero to nobody."

And again that big, tough, belligerent guy (we told him later that he had become *our* hero) spoke up, "I done tol' you, Man, you *my* hero. You the only one of us brave enough to tell that story the other day. You *my* hero."

"Yeah, that's right. That's right, Man," the rest chimed. "You can't say you not a hero."

This time, the atmosphere was casual. The kids seemed comfortable offering support to one another; no dramatic pauses ensued. It seemed that a new standard for behavior towards one another had been set, and that peer-affirmation would now be the rule, rather than the exception, with this group.

On later visits, counselors confirmed that this was so. There had been fewer reprimands for verbal and physical abuse; more instances of what the counselors termed "compassion." The same kinds of results, though less dramatic, were being reported throughout the program. Jim Maley, Director of Alaska Children's Services later wrote that the sessions "brought out the innocence of childhood, the questioning of youth, and the enthusiasm and joy of being a child. They really made the kids think."

In our modern society, kids don't often witness the "cool" guys being kind and caring. On television, the put-down has become an artform. Characters who are supposed to be friends constantly insult and verbally attack one another. TV families are even more dysfunctional, with parents and kids in constant verbal battles. It's all supposed to be terribly cool and witty. But kids copy the behavior modeled by their TV peers. In the classroom and in the halls, teachers witness the results: rudeness and violence to friend and foe alike. Kids are inculcated with the belief that if they show kindness, they will pay a price. They will be uncool. They'll be vulnerable. They won't fit in.

We believe that allowing kids to *experience* being kind and caring in a safe environment—one in which everyone is going to behave in that same way—is the key. When students trust that the rules will be enforced, and that they will not "lose respect" by being nice, they will begin to support and affirm each other. And when they find out how good it feels to be supportive and receive support in return, they will offer support more often. It's habit-forming!

Recently, we taught a residency in a multicultural middle school, with four core groups each consisting of thirty-five sixth, seventh, and eighth graders. Middle school kids are at a notoriously difficult age. They're awkward, vulnerable, self-conscious, and egocentric. Eager to be cool, they try to appear cynical and sophisticated. They are quick to identify, label, and attack weakness in each other, and are terrified of being the one attacked.

When we explained to the lead teachers that the participating students would each tell a story in front of the group on the final day of the class, and that the group would be required to listen attentively and to provide positive feedback, the instructors sneered in disbelief. "Not these kids. It might work in elementary school, but not here. They'll eat each other alive."

We assured them that it *would* work, and explained our methodology. They sneered some more. We smiled and invited them all to attend the final performance.

On performance day, each group assembled with palpable trepidation and dressed in their best. As they waited for the session to begin, we overheard groups of two and three students rehearsing and coaching one another (with positive comments). We reminded them of the order of the day, as described above, then called the first name.

The first teller rose. He was a chubby, rather effeminate young man who had been somewhat ostracized—last chosen for pairs and small-group activities, often seated alone. But all of the kids clapped as he "took the stage," and they met his eyes as he surveyed the audience. He was really good—animated, articulate, even flamboyant. The audience laughed *with* him, not at him, and they cheered when he took his bow. Then we asked for comments, and all the hands went up. The students praised his story, his voices, his gestures, his sound effects. Not a single guffaw or snort was heard; there were no rolling eyes, no sarcasm. The magic had begun.

One by one, our tellers performed for each other. Some were astonishingly good, and some were pretty bad—but were obviously trying. No matter, the audience listened with rapt attention, responding to each effort with encouraging, positive comments. As a whole, they waited patiently and respectfully while a teller paused painfully trying to remember a forgotten line; they sat silent and still to hear a shy voice that could barely be heard. They never had to be begged to provide comments, leaving a teller standing in dismay. The comments were immediately forthcoming and obviously genuine.

The lead teachers were stunned. Two told us later that they had wiped tears from their eyes. "It gave me goosebumps when they told each other what they liked about the story. I thought they would rag on each other, but they actually seemed eager to find something good to say. I never thought they could do it."

But they had done it, and witnessing that had changed the teachers' perspectives. The teachers themselves became a little less cynical about their students, and began to expect—and therefore receive—better behavior from them. In a letter from one of the teachers, we were thrilled to read,

I was pleasantly surprised at the students' positive response. Those students who would typically not give into being "up

148

front" and "out there" in public speaking began to relax bit by bit. Great experience!

I believe teachers may be the hardest group to reach, teach, or entertain, me included. Thankfully, I let myself get drawn into your experiences and knowledge and had a wonderful time. For the first time in a long time, I saw a bit of color creeping into my educational and personal life. I realized that I love to tell stories, either written or oral, and that I think my life out in story form. It was great fun to see a new side of my cynical old self.

Not only do students gain from the process of learning to tell, but they gain from the experience of telling to others. In California, teacher Kevin Cordi has formed a storytelling troupe called *Voices of Illusion*, which sponsors storytelling events and performs for young and old alike. They have told for small groups of senior citizens, for large-scale conferences, for preschoolers, and for their peers. Still, the most important audience, reports Kevin, are the students themselves.

I have watched how quickly a sense of group cohesion builds from not only youth telling stories, but youth listening to stories, and from this exchange other youth build ideas for stories, and youth begin loving stories. In this environment, a real sense of community grows; a community that cares about each other and a community that shares with one another. This community creates a positive sense of value; the value for the growth of not only a person's story, but the person. My students truly care about the nature and nurture of the other student tellers. They are helpful and create a non-threatening environment to grow; a place for which I am truly thankful.

These young tellers have a deep understanding of story's reach, both in their lives and in the lives of their listeners. Cordi helped us collect comments from the troupe on their experiences. Here are some examples:

Storytelling is a very powerful teaching tool, because it holds people's attention, while teaching them at the same time.

—KEVIN SHUKLIAN

Stories teach me morals and values. My Sadako story is great because you learn from it educationally and also morally.

—DAWN ESCOBAR

Storytelling can tell and teach many things, from the use of drugs to a crazy aunt of the family. People don't really know that storytelling has the power to make someone cry of sadness or cry from laughter and Voices of Illusion is one of the many ways to show that power.

—KEN AROLA

150

Stories open up new windows for thinking for the teller and the listener.

—LACY CHAFFIN

Stories are very powerful. You can learn from the characters' mistakes. You learn a lesson and are entertained at the same time.

—ANN CANO

I learned that our stories teach us how to be more creative, peaceful and especially how to use words with more care. With stories you can see from all sides and not just one. It also gives you more chance to know and see the background of other people and see where they come from.

—NICOLE DURKIN

Yes, experience really *is* the best teacher. Experience it for yourself and you'll see.

4
Making It Work

Creating an Atmosphere of Caring

If you model the behavior, you don't have to post the rules.[1]

—PEYTON WILLIAMS

It's no surprise that shaping children who will do what's right is easier in an environment where being honest, decent, and caring is perceived to be the norm—what everybody simply expects of everybody else. But that environment is not easy to achieve.

Several years ago, we watched as two teachers demonstrated a complete lack of respect for each other and for their students. While participating in an "Arts for Character Education" program at a local school, we watched as classes filed into the media center for the storytelling session. One teacher shoved to the front of the group and squeezed herself and her children into the front row. A few minutes later, another teacher brought her class to the front, and stood, arms akimbo, staring at the first teacher.

"What are you doing with your class in the front?" she bellowed. "You know that my class always sits in the front for assemblies!"

Her co-worker looked away insolently, but responded just as loudly, "Yeah, I know your class always gets the best seats, but we got here first this time, so you just take your little class to the back."

"I don't think so," the second teacher retorted. "You're going to move your class."

"No, I am not. Now, you just move on back." She still wouldn't look at the other speaker.

The other teachers joined in at this point and urged the late-arriving class to settle in the back so that the session could begin. The teacher complied, but not quietly. All the way to the back, she continued to complain loudly about the other teacher. Meanwhile, the teacher in the front row gestured and postured and exhorted, "That's right, you just move on back!"

The word of the week at that school was "POLITENESS."

It's hard to believe that any number of lessons on the meaning of that word could have been more powerful than what the teachers were modeling. In an atmosphere where adults treat each other with open disrespect, it's no wonder that children act disrespectfully to each other and to their teachers.

Unfortunately, this is not an isolated incident. Our children are surrounded by negative examples—on television, in the street, in the marketplace, and too often, in the classroom and in the home. We preach tolerance and practice intolerance. We tell kids to be patient, yet we demonstrate our frustration at delays with words and actions.

153

Storytelling as Character-Education Model

In a perfect world, children would be surrounded by examples of peaceful co-existence, honesty, respect, and responsibility. We can certainly work towards that goal, encouraging others to join us. But in the world we currently have, it is up to each of us as individuals to provide that "moral environment" which will nurture the moral child.

What can a storyteller—whether teacher-storyteller, parent-storyteller, or professional—actually do?

PROVIDE AN EXAMPLE OF LEADERSHIP FROM THE TOP.

In character-education literature, the phrase "moral leadership" refers to proactive leading by principals, directors, or superintendents. This is the best-case scenario, but not always the reality. We suggest that *you* provide that leadership, no matter what you perceive your true position to be within the organization. If you are the janitor, a concerned mom, or a visiting storyteller, you can be the impetus for positive change within your sphere of influence.

Seek out training opportunities for yourself and for others in character education. Find out what groups are actively promoting values education in your community, and join them. Read the literature, and encourage others to do the same by lending your books, leaving them conveniently in the staff room, or providing bibliographic citations or photocopies. If others won't take the time to read, at least talk with them—in a nonconfrontational manner—about what you've read, and share your enthusiasm and optimism for success.

If you are a visiting storyteller, provide teachers with bibliographies of appropriate tales to share, and with information about other tellers in the area who can offer character-education storytelling programs. (Your willingness to share this will in itself provide a character lesson.)

As a parent, you can provide a role-model within your neighborhood and within your PTA. A formal character-education curriculum may not be the answer for your community, but modeling and discussing shared values always is.

FOSTER DISCIPLINE THAT MODELS, PROMOTES, AND UPHOLDS VALUES THROUGHOUT THE CHILD'S ENVIRONMENT.

How rules are set up and enforced makes all the difference in how seriously kids take them—and whether a rule violation becomes an occasion for a student's moral growth.

Teachers know that if they ask children to help them identify appropriate behaviors for the classroom, the kids will name those which are also important to the teacher. Likewise, students can unerringly spot inappropriate behaviors, and can help develop disciplinary actions they feel are justified and fair. When teachers grant students "ownership" of classroom behaviors, the young people understand the rules and are likely to abide by them. When rules are broken, the class knows what to expect.

As a visiting storyteller, you may feel that you have very little say in discipline, but that's not necessarily so. First, it's important to tailor the space as much as possible to create a good environment for storytelling—and, in that way, to create the best possible experience for everyone. What does this have to do with discipline? Almost everything.

If the children are so crowded that they can't get comfortable, they will wiggle and be disruptive. If they are facing the light, with you as the storyteller backlit, they will not be able to see you and will start to look away, get distracted, and become disruptive. If they can't hear, can't see, or can't concentrate because of too much distraction in their surroundings, they will become disruptive. Get the picture?

When you make arrangements, ask about the space you will be using and tell the contact person your optimal requirements. You will need a place where the children's backs are to the window or doors, where they will be seated comfortably, and where they will be able to hear without distortion and see without contortions. Be aware of how many listeners you are comfortable with at a time (this will depend of the age of the children, the number of other adults present, the quality of the sound system, and your own experience). Try to limit the audience size to one you can control and relate to.

You can also help faculty and students alike understand what is acceptable behavior during your storytelling session. We've tried sending pre-site packets that include this information, and sometimes it's effective. But too often, it's overlooked or used to bludgeon the students. We've all heard some principals and teachers blast the children with negative expectations: "You people had better sit down, shut up, and listen or out you go!" YUCK!

We prefer positive expectations, and we've found that children will rise to the level you expect of them. So we might say something like, "I can tell you're going to be a great audience! What do you think "being a great audience" means?" Then we ask the kids to help define what a great audience is. We get answers like "Be really quiet" and "We gotta listen" (which we supplement with "And I might ask you to help out with the story, so then I DON'T want you to be quiet, okay? But you'll have to listen so you know when I need you"). That kind of introduction helps both students and teachers understand your expectations and prepare to meet them. Then the kids can prove you right by being a truly great audience! (Please note: if the stories aren't well chosen, or well presented, you can't expect well-behaved listeners. It's up to you to do your part, too.)

One note about the "Shut up and sit down" introduction. We all experience it at one time or another, and it's important to dispel the negative impact of that warning without "dissing" the one who gave it. Some tellers simply look and act so differently from the introducer that the children immediately sense change is in the air. (A slouchy walk, a silly entrance, a style of dress, might help you accomplish this if you are interested in giving it a try.) But we find that simply saying, "Mr. Brown was right about needing to be quiet during storytelling. But sometimes, I might need for you to be noisy, or silly, too. You'll know when that is. And of course, you can laugh when it's funny and clap when it's good, okay? Now . . ." That acknowledges the intentions of the introduction while re-setting the parameters for behavior.

And don't mistake enthusiasm for disruptiveness. After a story that excites the audience, you'll get a wonderful (and loud) buzz of sound—kids imitating the sound effects, or laughing about a character's mishaps, or simply telling each other, "That was so cool!" This buzz threatens many teachers (and some storytellers), who think that the kids are getting out of control. But just the opposite is true—when the kids are that excited about a story, they will settle down immediately when you begin the next one. After all, they don't want to miss any of the action.

As a parent telling stories within the family, you can apply the same concepts. Find the optimal storytelling/read-aloud site in your home and the best time to share the stories. Let your children know how high your opinion is of their listening ability. Choose stories that you know will appeal to their emotional and intellectual needs. And if the results aren't always perfect, look first at the environment rather than the child for the reasons.

CREATE A MORAL ATMOSPHERE OF MUTUAL RESPECT, FAIRNESS, AND COOPERATION IN ALL RELATIONSHIPS.

Remember those publicly warring teachers at the "Arts for Character Education" program? They were certainly not providing a moral atmosphere of mutual respect. But even in the face of poor adult behavior, you can create the right atmosphere for yourself and your audience. Thank the children for waiting patiently and quietly while everyone got settled. Acknowledge how hard it is to sit on that hard, cold floor, and tell them you're proud of their cooperation.

Even if all the children aren't exhibiting good behavior, acknowledging those who *are* is important. For one thing, it tells them that their good behavior is not in vain; for another, it helps those who are misbehaving understand what you expect without making them wrong. Saying, "Wow! Some of you are really doing a great job of waiting quietly and patiently" is so much better than saying, "All of you get quiet right this minute." If you do need to ask for quiet, do it with a smile, a whisper into the microphone, and a gesture, rather than a shriek. The shriek only adds to the din and provides a negative example.

Between stories, be aware of the "teachable moments." If there was audience participation, you can comment on the good teamwork and cooperation, making the story even more fun. After quiet stories, you can point out how considerate everyone is being, listening quietly so that others can hear. By helping them recognize their own good qualities, you show them respect, and you will get respect in return.

Before and after the program, you also have opportunities to show the children how much you respect them. Greet students as they settle in; make eye contact; smile. As the group leaves, shake hands or wave or simply nod—but don't ignore the young people. Through stories, the children feel connected to you. Ignoring them after the stories are finished makes kids feel disconnected and cheated. Do your part to create an environment of mutual respect by acknowledging your listeners and matching their enthusiasm with your own.

Selecting Stories for Character Education

We hope that you've already noticed that the stories in this book are not a collection of prissy Victorian morality tales. They are lively, irreverent, funny, and action-packed! They are stories that are engaging and challenging and provoking.

If you have recently been reading some of the Victorian tales of virtue and found them not to your liking, you may have turned away from the idea of storytelling as a tool for character education. But there is such a treasury of world tales from which to choose! Among them, you will surely find something which suits your taste, and which captivates the children as well.

Again, we stress that it's important to select stories appropriate to your audience's emotional and intellectual needs. We've given some indication of grade levels and appropriateness for the stories in this book, but there is no hard-and-fast rule about such things. You have to know your audience, and choose stories that you feel will best match their needs.

There are two important points to keep in mind about appropriateness: first, *you* must like the story in order to share it well. Even if the tale is perfect for the intended audience and provides just the right moral lesson, it is not the right one to tell if you don't like it. Storytelling is such a personal artform that you share your attitude about a tale as you share the story—and if your attitude is a negative one, that is the attitude your listeners will have as well.

Second, until about eighth grade, children's listening and emotional comprehension is about two grade levels higher than their reading comprehension. This allows you to choose stories that they may not be able to read for themselves.

Some general information about child development related to story-telling and reading aloud may help you in making your decisions. Remember that all child-development charts are approximations. Children progress at their own rates, and the development is continuous through phases that merge into one another and overlap.

Infants (0–18 months)

- like action nursery rhymes
- fall asleep to nursery songs and lullabies
- listen to Mother Goose as they are rocked
- imitate action
- participate in animal sounds
- relate to real life
- like to see babies in books
- like the 3 Rs: rhythm, repetition, rhyme

Toddlers (18–36 months)

- like to hear the same stories over and over
- repeat Mother Goose by heart
- explore the world through their senses: taste, smell, touch
- like short rhyming stories
- like large, clear, realistic pictures
- like to name and identify objects/pictures

Preschoolers (3–4 years)

- use words to express themselves
- struggle for independence: "I wanna do it myself!"
- play with language: sing-song, nonsense sounds
- are fascinated by other children but share grudgingly
- are fearful of the dark and strangers
- like simple folktales but not fairytales
- like to fill in the gaps: "Humpty Dumpty sat on the _____"
- like predictability

160

- like to repeat phrases and actions
- have short attention spans

5-year-olds (kindergarten)

- like stories with animals that talk
- like simple folktales and some fairytales
- like a prince and princess in the story
- believe in magic
- think fairy tale characters really lived a long time ago
- sometimes confuse real and make-believe

6-year-olds (1st grade)

- still like fairytales
- like being read to/told to
- memorize poetry and nonsense (patterned language)
- still sometimes confuse real and make-believe
- are developing a growing sense of independence but need security
- still have fears of monsters, strangers, dark

7-year-olds (2nd grade)

- seek acceptance by other children their age
- show increasing independence of home and family
- understand more complex stories than they can read
- see the world as good/bad; fair/unfair
- believe in magic
- accept fairytale "eye for an eye" morality and cruel justice

8-year-olds (3rd grade)

- reach peak of interest in fairytales
- begin interest in stories of real life (and nonfiction generally)
- like poetry/verse, riddles, jokes, off-the-wall humor, gross stuff
- think picture books are babyish

9-year-olds (4th grade)

- are fascinated with "strange but true"
- like mysteries

- prefer tall tales over fairytales
- like happy endings
- have a weird sense of humor
- like gross stuff, corny jokes

10-year-olds (5th grade)

- are satisfied with themselves
- like adventure with real heroes
- like funny books and stories (such as *How to Eat Fried Worms*)
- are gender-oriented (think in terms of "boy" stories and "girl" stories)

11- and 12-year-olds (pre-teens; 6th and 7th grade)

- interested in opposite sex
- interested in fads; often like popular music (rock, rap, etc.)
- like HORROR stories
- feel intense peer pressure
- memorize song lyrics
- like horse stories, survival stories, adventures
- like happy endings
- begin to like sci-fi
- like to be cool

12 and up

- like HORROR, comedy, fantasy, sci-fi
- like mythology; relate to metaphor
- like to be cool

In addition to the bibliographies included in the back of this book, we offer some stories for particular age groups. These are suggestions only. Many tales can be told to a much wider age range than our list indicates:

Preschool (ages 3-5)

Harrison, Annette. *Easy-to-Tell Stories for Young Children*. National Storytelling Press, 1992.

Hutchinson, Veronica S. *Chimney Corner Stories: Tales for Little Children.* Linnett Books, 1992.

Richardson, Frederick. *Great Children's Stories.* Rand McNally & Co., 1972.

Sierra, Judy, and Robert Kaminski. *Multicultural Folktales: Stories to Tell Young Children.* The Oryx Press, 1991.

Sierra, Judy. *Nursery Tales Around the World.* Clarion, 1996.

K-2 grade (Primary/Elementary)

MacDonald, Margaret Read. *Twenty Tellable Tales: Audience Participation Folktales for the Beginning Storyteller.* H.W. Wilson, 1986.

Tashjian, Virginia. *Juba This and Juba That: Story Hour Stretches for Large and Small Groups.* Little, Brown, 1969.

———. *With a Deep Sea Smile: Story Hours Stretches for Large and Small Groups.* Little, Brown, 1974.

3-4 grade (Intermediate)

Lester, Julius. *Tales of Uncle Remus: The Adventures of Brer Rabbit.* Dial, 1988. (Also see the others in this series.)

Chase, Richard. *The Grandfather Tales.* Houghton Mifflin, 1990.

———. *The Jack Tales.* Houghton Mifflin, 1943.

Milord, Susan. *Tales Alive! Ten Multicultural Folktales with Activities.* Williamson Publishing, 1995.

Del Negro, Janice. "Stories for Grades Three and Up." In *Tales as Tools: The Power of Story In the Classroom.* National Storytelling Press, 1994, pp. 206-209.

Middle School

Brunvand, Jan Harold. *Curses! Broiled Again! The Hottest Urban Legends Going.* Norton, 1989.

Cohen, Daniel. *Southern Fried Rat and Other Gruesome Tales.* Avon, 1983.

Hamilton, Virginia. *The People Could Fly: American Black Folktales.* Knopf, 1985.

———. *In the Beginning: Creation Stories from Around the World.* Harcourt, Brace, Jovanovich, 1988.

Haven, Kendall. "Stories that Appeal to Older Children." In *Tales as Tools: The Power of Story in the Classroom.* National Storytelling Press, 1994, p. 208.

High School

Bierce, Ambrose. "A Cold Night." Adapted by Craig Roney in *Tales as Tools: The Power of Story in the Classroom.* National Storytelling Press, 1994, pp. 120-22.
Babbitt, Natalie. *The Devil's Storybook.* Farrar, Straus & Giroux, 1974.
Reader's Digest. *Great Short Stories of the World, 1972.*

You may be asking, "But how do I choose the appropriate story for *character education?*" Well, after due consideration, we believe there's really no such thing as a story that doesn't have a moral lesson. For instance, while it's not easy to see any immediate moral lesson in the story of the Gingerbread Boy, Judy Driscoll's article, "Truth in a Gingerbread Man,"[2] helped us see the possibilities. This rap version grew from reading her piece:

THE GINGERBREAD BOY RAP
by Sherry Norfolk

Did you ever feel that things were falling apart,
At school, at home, in affairs of the heart?
Did you ever think about running away
To solve your problems? Well, here's what I say:
There once was a dude who was made of dough—
Gingerbread, if you want to know.
He was cute and tasty but he didn't wanna be!
He wanted, he needed, he had to be *free.*
So he took off one day, away from his woes.
He ran away, straight to his foes.
Here's the tale—it's sad but true—
And the very same thing could happen to you
If you run and hide instead of face up

To your problems—FACE 'em—You gotta be tough!
Listen up! Hear the tale of this jerk
Who thought that running away would work.
Well, the Gingerbread Boy was made by Gran.
She patted him and shaped him, and put him in a pan.
She baked him brown and set him to cool
On the windowsill—now she was a fool!
'Cause he heard her say to the little old man,
"We'll eat him for dinner just as soon as we can!"
"Whoa! Trouble ahead! I gotta scram from here!"
So he upped and fled, didn't think, you hear?
Now he didn't know anything about a plan.
He didn't have a map, didn't know the land.
But he thought he was cool, so as he ran
He called, "Run, run, as fast as you can!
"You can't catch me, I'm the Gingerbread Man!"
The little old lady and the little old man
Set out to catch him, but away he ran!
He passed a horse and he passed a cow.
And he outran 'em—I don't know how.
He passed a pig—a fat old thang.
And to each and every one he sang,
"Run, run, as fast as you can!
"You can't catch me, I'm the Gingerbread Man!"
Well, the little old woman and the little old man,
The horse, the cow and the pig, they ran!
They chased that boy till he came to a stream
And they came to a halt to enjoy the scene.
See, a fox sat waiting at the water there.
He said to the boy, "Now don't you dare!
"The water's deep and you can't swim.
"Climb on my back." Now, my boy was dim!
He climbed on up and they started across.
And the fox said, "Move on up, or you'll be lost!"

165

That boy moved closer to the fox's jaws
Then the fox went SNAP!—that fox was boss.
He ate the boy with a mighty slurp.
He licked his lips, and he gave a burp.
Now that boy and I, we learned a lesson that day.
You gotta face your problems, you can't run away.
There's troubles everywhere, so you might as well face 'em.
Cause more will always come to replace 'em.
Don't run, run as fast as you can,
Or you'll end up like the Gingerbread Man!

Sometimes it's not obvious, and usually it doesn't come neatly phrased at the end of the tale, but all stories teach us something. When the lesson doesn't jump out, try asking yourself a few questions about the story:

Why did the characters behave as they did? Motivations such as greed or love or selfishness or generosity may become more obvious under careful scrutiny. (Think about the Gingerbread Boy—why he ran, why the others chased him, why he listened to the fox.)

What created the conflict in the story? If there was danger, was it caused by carelessness or stupidity or hunger? (Think about the Three Pigs—did the danger occur because the wolf was greedy or because he was hungry? Did the pigs get into danger because they were ignorant or just too lazy to build well?)

What were the turning points? When did the characters have chances to change the course of events—and what caused them to make the decisions they did? (Think about Little Red Riding Hood—what would have happened if she had chosen to listen to her mother's advice and not talk to strangers? Why do you think she talked to that strange wolf, anyhow?)

As you ask these questions and think about the answers, you will discover many lessons within the stories you read and tell.

Preparing to Tell Stories for Character Education

First of all, we need to remind ourselves that we tell stories in the same way, whether for character-education purposes or for a birthday party. The plots must be clear and the images vivid no matter *why* we're telling. Keeping that in mind, we have some suggestions for making the character-education experience a positive one.

After reading the stories in this book, you already know that we believe in making the storytelling experience fun. In so many of the character-education curricula that we have seen, the lessons are boring, pedantic, didactic, and preachy. But storytelling for character education doesn't have to be that way. Folktales don't require the solemnity of sermons to make them vivid and memorable. They teach their lessons subtly, often with laughter, sometimes tongue-in-cheek, always leaving something open to interpretation. All this makes the stories such powerful learning tools because listeners can derive what they need when they're ready, both emotionally and intellectually.

So . . . here are a few final dos and don'ts that we'd like to share with you:

> *Do* find a story you love.
> *Don't* expect everyone to like every story you prefer.
> *Do* identify the character-education lessons within the story,
>   *but* . . .
> *Don't* expect everyone to see the same lessons you do. We all
>   have different emotional and intellectual levels, and the
>   story will go where it is needed.

Don't beat kids over the head with the moral. Let them find
it for themselves.

Do engage the listeners in activities and discussions that help
them grasp the meaning of the story.

Don't discuss every story you tell. That takes the fun out, and
children begin to dread the storytelling rather than looking forward to it.

And finally,

Do remember that it's important to let the students express
their opinions without being made "right" or "wrong."

Don't judge contributions to the discussion. Pay attention,
listen, and allow all viewpoints to be expressed and
respected.

Don't say NO—ask WHY!

Endnotes

INTRODUCTION

1. Kevin Ryan, "Mining the Values in the Curriculum," *Educational Leadership*, November 1993, p. 17.
2. Josephson Institute of Ethics, http://www.josephsoninstitute.org/quotes/quoteeducation.htm
3. John Dewey, "Character Training for Youth" (1934). Quoted from *the Character Page* (http://www.neiu.edu/~ccunning/chared/), assembled by Craig A. Cunningham, Northwestern Illinois University.
4. C.S. Lewis, *The Abolition of Man* (Macmillan, 1947).
5. Thomas Lickona, handouts for Character Education Workshop, Gwinnet County, GA, March 1997.
6. Lickona, *Educating for Values and Character: How Our Schools Can Teach Respect and Responsibility* (Bantam, 1991), 21.
7. Robert Coles, *The Moral Intelligence of Children* (Random House, 1997), 5.
8. Quoted from Joe Hayes, in a presentation at the MISD Storytelling Festival, Dec. 7, 1996.
9. Quoted from Ruthilde M. Kronberg, *Clever Folk: Tales of Wisdom, Wit and Wonder* (Libraries Unlimited, 1993), ix.
10. William J. Bennett. *The Moral Compass: a Companion to the Book of Virtues* (Simon and Schuster, 1995), 12–13.
11. Ryan, "Mining the Values," 17.
12. Lickona, *Educating for Values*, 79–81.
13. *The Heartwood Ethics Curriculum* is published by the Heartwood Institute (12300 Perry Hwy, Wexford, PA).
14. Michael Caduto and Joe Bruchac, *Keepers of the Earth* (Fulcrum Publishing, 1988), 4.
15. Fran Stallings, "Honesty, Respect, Compassion: Strengthening Character through Stories," *Storytelling Magazine*, January 1997, 24.

169

ONE: GETTING READY

Before You Begin

1. Margaret Read MacDonald, *The Storyteller's Start-up Book: Finding, Learning, Performing, and Using Folktales* (August House, 1993), 44.
2. Susan Strauss, *The Passionate Fact: Storytelling in Natural History and Cultural Interpretation* (Fulcrum Publishing, 1996), 2–3.

Help! I'm Not a Storyteller!

1. Jean Grasso Fitzpatrick, *Once Upon a Family: Read-Aloud Stories and Activities That Nurture Healthy Kids* (Viking, 1998), 57.

TWO: THE STORIES

The Dancing Hyena

1. General Colin Powell, "Everybody's Children: Giving Helps Young People Grow," *Time*, December 15, 1997, p. 135.

Bibi and the Singing Drum

1. Fitzpatrick, *Once Upon a Family*, 18.

THREE: STORYTELLING AS AN EXPERIENTIAL APPROACH TO CHARACTER EDUCATION

1. Coles, *Moral Intelligence*, 16.
2. "The Little Girl and the Gunniwolf," Motif K606 *Escape by singing a song. Captive gradually moves away and finally escapes.*

FOUR: MAKING IT WORK

1. Peyton Williams, from an address at the Character Education Workshop, Gwinnet County, GA, March 1997. (Williams is assistant superintendent for Georgia's Department of Education.)
2. Judy Driscoll, "Truth in a Gingerbread Man," *Christian Library Journal*, January 1996, pp. 13–14.

Bibliographies

RESOURCES ON CHARACTER EDUCATION

For Educators:

Benninga, Jacques S., ed. *Moral, Character and Civic Education in the Elementary School.* Teachers College Press, 1991.

Cohen, Philip. "The Content of Their Character." *Curriculum Update,* Spring 1995, unpaged. (Newsletter available from the Association for Supervision and Curriculum Development.)

Hartjen, Raymond H. *Empowering the Child: Nurturing the Hungry Mind.* Alternative Education Press, Ltd., 1994.

Kohn, Alfie. "How Not to Teach Values: a Critical Look at Character Education." *Phi Delta Kappan,* Feb. 1997, pp. 428–39.

Lickona, Thomas. *Educating for Character: How Our Schools Can Teach Respect and Responsibility.* Bantam Books, 1991.

Mecca, Marilyn E. "Classrooms Where Children Learn to Care." *Childhood Education,* Winter 1995/96, pp. 72–74.

Rosenblatt, Roger. "Teaching Johnny to be Good." *The New York Times Magazine,* April 30, 1995, pp. 36–41.

Ryan, Kevin. "It's Back to Basics, But Teachers Haven't Gotten the Word." *Journal of Teacher Education,* September-October 1994, pp. 303–305.

Vessels, Gordon. *Character and Community Development: A School Planning and Teacher Training Handbook.* Greenwood Publishing, 1998.

For Parents:

Bar-Levav, Reuvan. *Every Family Needs a CEO: What Mothers and Fathers Can Do About Our Deteriorating Families and Values.* Fathering, Inc. Press, 1995.

Coles, Robert. *The Moral Intelligence of Children.* Random House, 1997.

Collins, Marva. *Values, Lighting the Candle of Excellence: A Practical Guide for the Family.* Dove Audio, 1996.

Dosick, Wayne D. *Golden Rules: the Ten Ethical Values Parents Need to Teach Their Children.* HarperCollins, 1995.

Fitzpatrick, Jean Grasso. *Once Upon a Family: Read-Aloud Stories and Activities that Nurture Healthy Kids.* Viking, 1998.

Lickona, Thomas. *Raising Good Children from Birth through the Teenage Years*. Bantam Books, 1992.

Rosenberg, Debra. "Raising a Moral Child." *Newsweek* (Special Edition Supplement), Spring 1997, pp. 92–93.

Wray, Herbert. "The Moral Child." *U.S. New and World Report*, June 3, 1996, pp. 52–59.

FURTHER READING ABOUT STORYTELLING, LITERATURE, AND CHARACTER EDUCATION

Andrews, Sharon Vincz. *Teaching Kids to Care: Exploring Values through Literature and Inquiry*. ERIC / Edinfo Press, 1994.

Coles, Robert. *The Call of Stories: Teaching and the Moral Imagination*. Houghton Mifflin, 1989.

Cunningham, Marge. "The Moral of the Story." *Storytelling*, Spring 1993, pp. 9–12.

Gibbs, Linda J. and Edward J Earley. *Developing Values Through Children's Literature*. Phi Delta Kappan Education Foundation, 1994.

Lamme, Linda, et al. *Literature-Based Character Education*. Oryx Press, 1992.

Marinelli, Stacie. "Getting Kids High on Life." *Storytelling*, Spring 1993, pp. 20–21.

National Storytelling Association. "Using Stories to Teach about Peace and the Environment." In *Tales as Tools: The Power of Story in the Classroom*. National Storytelling Press, 1994, pp. 100–114.

Paley, Vivian. *You Can't Say You Can't Play*. Harvard University Press, 1992.

Smith, Malcolm L. "Waging Peace in the Classroom." *Storytelling*, January 1997, pp. 12–16.

Stallings, Fran. "Honesty, Respect, Compassion: Strengthening Character through Stories." *Storytelling*, January 1997, pp. 24–29.

"V is for Virtue." *Copycat*, May/June 1996, pp. 14–17.

Wilson, James Q. "Tales of Virtue: Moral Development and Children." *Current*, September 1994, pp. 4–8.

CHARACTER-BUILDING STORIES RECOMMENDED BY EDUCATORS AND STORYTELLERS

The following bibliographies are in no way intended to be exhaustive! We have included those stories and collections which we have found to be the most useful in our own work, and those which have been recommended to us by teachers, parents, and other storytellers. We hope that these suggestions will lead you to discover your own favorites.

Grouping the stories according to virtue is tricky at best. While we have indicated the virtue that is most strongly illustrated by a particular tale, we certainly don't intend to limit the use or application of these or any other stories by this categorization.

General Collections

Abrahams, Roger D., ed. *Afro-American Folktales: Stories from Black Traditions in the New World.* Pantheon, 1985. (See Part III. "Getting a Comeuppance: How (and How Not) to Act Stories.")

Aesop's Fables. Any edition.

Bennett, William J. *The Book of Virtues: a Treasury of Great Moral Stories.* Simon & Schuster, 1993.

_____. *The Moral Compass: Stories for a Life's Journey.* Simon & Schuster, 1995.

Brody, Ed, Jay Goldspinner, Katie Green, Rona Leventhal, and John Porcino, eds. *Spinning Tales, Weaving Hope: Stories of Peace, Justice, and the Environment.* New Society, 1992.

Cole, Joanna, ed. *Best-Loved Folktales of the World.* Anchor Books, 1982. (See "Fables and Tales with a Moral," in the Index of Categories of Tales, p. 783.)

Creeden, Sharon. *Fair is Fair: World Folktales of Justice.* August House, 1994.

Daphne Muse, ed. *Prejudice: Stories about Hate, Ignorance, Revelation, and Transformation.* Hyperion, 1995.

Forest, Heather. *Wisdom Tales from Around the World: Fifty Gems of Story and Wisdom from such Diverse Traditions as Sufi, Zen, Taoist, Christian, Jewish, Buddhist, African and Native American.* August House, 1996.

Greer, Colin, and Herbert Kohl, eds. *A Call to Character: A Family Treasury of Stories, Poems, Plays, Proverbs and Fables to Guide the Development of Values for You and Your Children.* HarperCollins, 1995.

Kronberg, Ruthilde M. *Clever Folk: Tales of Wisdom, Wit, and Wonder.* Libraries Unlimited, Inc., 1993.

Lobel, Arnold. *Fables.* Harper & Row, 1980.

MacDonald, Margaret Read. *Look Back and See: Twenty Lively Tales for Gentle Tellers.* H. W. Wilson, 1991.

Stern, Anita. *Tales from Many Lands: an Anthology of Multicultural Folk Literature.* National Textbook Company, 1996.

Peace: Living in harmony with one another

Aesop. "The Lion and the Mouse," *Aesop's Fables*. Any edition.

"The Cow-Tail Switch." In Courlander, Harold, and George Herzog. *The Cow-Tail Switch and Other West African Stories*. Holt, 1949.

"The North Wind and the Sun." In Harrison, Annette. *Easy-to-Tell Stories for Young Children*. National Storytelling Press, 1992.

Courtesy, Kindness, and Compassion: Treating others as you yourself would like to be treated

Freedman, Florence B., reteller. *Brothers: A Hebrew Legend*. Harper, 1985.

"Gallymanders! Gallymanders!" In Smith, Jimmy Neil. *Why the Possum's Tail is Bare and Other Classic Southern Stories*. Avon, 1993.

"I'm Tipingee, She's Tipengee, We're Tipingee, Too." In Wolkstein, Diane. *The Magic Orange Tree and Other Haitian Folktales*. Knopf, 1978.

MacDonald, Margaret Read. *Peace Tales: World Folktales to Talk About*. Linnett, 1992.

"Medio Pollito." In Jennings, Linda. *A Treasury of Stories from Around the World*. Kingfisher Books, 1993.

Honesty: A willingness to say openly what is known to be true

Andersen, Hans Christian. *The Emperor's New Clothes*. Any edition.

Demi. *The Empty Pot*. Holt, 1990.

Jaffrey, Madhur. "Lakshmir and the Clever Washerwoman." In *A Treasury of Stories from Around the World."* Kingfisher Books, 1993.

Thomson, Peggy. *The King has Horse's Ears*. Simon & Schuster, 1988.

Work Ethic: Willingness to work to achieve a desired goal

Aesop. "Grasshopper and the Ant," *Aesop's Fables*. Any edition.

Galdone, Paul. *The Little Red Hen*. Seabury Press, 1973.

Hodges, Margaret. *The Hero of Bremen*. Holiday, 1993.

Teamwork and Cooperation: Being able to work with others to accomplish a task, play a game, etc.

Domanska, Janina. *The Turnip*. Macmillan, 1969.

"Harambee: The Story of the Pull-Together Morning." In Edwards, Carolyn McVickar. *Sun Stories: Tales from Around the World to Illuminate the Days and Nights of Our Lives*. HarperSanFrancisco, 1995.

McDermott, Gerald. *Anansi the Spider: a Tale from the Ashanti*. Holt, Rinehart and Winston, 1972.

"Why Hare is Always on the Run." In Milord, Susan. *Tales Alive! Ten Multicultural Folktales with Activities*. Williamson Publishing, 1995.

Humanity: Believing that people of different cultures, ages, abilities, religions, sexes, and races are equally valuable members of our society

"Kanu Above and Kanu Below." In MacDonald, Margaret Read. *The Storyteller's Start–up Book: Finding, Learning, Performing and Using Folktales*. August House, 1993.

"The Old Man and His Grandson." In Yolen, Jane, ed. *Favorite Folktales from around the World*. Random House, 1988.

Stamm, Claus. *Three Strong Women: a Tall Tale from Japan*. Viking Press, 1962.

"Why the Red Elf Cried." In Sakade, Florence, ed. *Urashima Taro and Other Japanese Children's Stories*. Charles E. Tuttle Company, 1959.

Andersen, Hans Christian. *"The Ugly Duckling."* Any edition.

Responsibility: A willingness to be accountable for your own actions without blaming others

Aardema, Verna. *Why Mosquitoes Buzz in People's Ears: a West African Folktale*. Dial Press, 1975.

Aesop. "The Boy Who Cried Wolf." In *Aesop's Fables*. Any edition.

Mosel, Arlene. *Tikki Tikki Tembo*. Holt, Rinehart and Winston, 1968.

"The Turkey Girl." In MacDonald, Margaret Read. *Look Back and See: Twenty Lively Tales for Gentle Tellers*. H.W. Wilson, 1991.

Respect: Showing regard for self, others, property, and those in authority

"Anansi and Turtle." In Young, Richard Alan, and Judy Dockery Young. *African-American Folktales for Young Readers*. August House, 1993.

"Knee-High Man." In Botkin, B.A., ed. *A Treasury of American Folklore: Stories, Ballads, and Traditions of the People*. Crown Publishers, 1944.

"Owl." In Wolkstein, Diane. *Magic Orange Tree and Other Haitian Folktales*. Knopf, 1978.

"The Skull in the Road." In Young, Richard Alan, and Judy Dockery Young. *The Scary Story Reader*. August House, 1993.

Gerson, Mary-Joan. *Why the Sky is Far Away: a Nigerian Folktale*. Little, Brown, 1974.